PAVLOV'S DOG

First published in Great Britain, Australia and New Zealand in 2018 by Modern Books
An imprint of Elwin Street Productions Limited
14 Clerkenwell Green
London EC1R 0DP
www.modern-books.com

Interior design and illustrations: Jason Anscomb, Rawshock design
Photo credits: Shutterstock.com 13, 14, 85, 127, 164.

ISBN 978-1-911130-32-1

10 9 8 7 6 5 4

Printed in China

PAVLOV'S DOG

AND 49 OTHER EXPERIMENTS
THAT REVOLUTIONISED PSYCHOLOGY

ADAM HART-DAVIS

(m)

Contents

Introduction

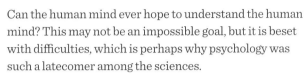

Can the human mind ever hope to understand the human mind? This may not be an impossible goal, but it is beset with difficulties, which is perhaps why psychology was such a latecomer among the sciences.

The ancient Greeks, Plato and Aristotle, wrote about the 'psyche'. Originally the word meant life, or breath, and later spirit or soul (Psyche being the goddess of the soul in Greek and Roman mythology). Now we use *psychology* to refer to all aspects of the human mind.

And what about that mind? In the sixteenth century the French philosopher René Descartes argued that the body and brain are machines, but we need a mind as well, to think, feel and make choices or decisions. This view is known as Cartesian dualism and it pervades almost all aspects of psychology. Even as very young children we feel as though there are thinking, conscious 'selves' inside our bodies. But the more we learn, the less plausible this seems to be, and right from the start psychology has struggled with this problem.

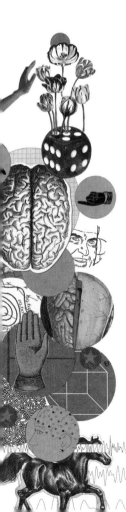

The first person to call himself a psychologist was Wilhelm Wundt, who founded a psychological research laboratory in Leipzig, Germany, in 1879. He is known as the father of experimental psychology (a branch of the science that focuses on empirical evidence gathered through experimentation rather than theory). The first textbook on the subject, William James's great *The Principles of Psychology*, appeared in 1890. The noted naturalist Charles Darwin didn't consider himself a psychologist, but he was captivated by what factors proved intelligence and made a 40-year study of the humble earthworm, and at the turn of the century Edward

Thorndike explored the degree to which animals could learn and reason.

The early twentieth century, saw the beginnings of 'behaviourism', which sought to explore only observable events using rigorous experimental methods and resist speculating about the subjective or invisible. In hindsight there were many ethical breaches in this period, and a number of studies remain highly controversial, but much was learned and the field psychology was greatly expanded by the likes of Ivan Pavlov and his discovery of classical conditioning.

Post-war, Jean Piaget's carried out groundbreaking studies of the cognitive development in children and Leon Festinger coined the notion of cognitive dissonance. The 1960s saw Stanley Milgram's obedience studies gain worldwide attention and in the 1970s Donald G. Dutton and Arthur P. Aron asked if there was a link between sexual attraction and fear. The science of psychology grew and grew, influencing numerous areas of our everyday lives.

In the following pages these great experiments, and many more besides, will carry us through the history of psychology as well as propelling us on a journey deep into the understanding of ourselves.

Adam Hart-Davis

CHAPTER 1: Beginnings:
1848-1919

The idea of psychology was barely conceived during the nineteenth century, but Charles Darwin's groundbreaking explorations roused a great curiosity in animal behaviour and what it might teach us about human beings. And after the publication of William James's *The Principles of Psychology* (1890) this curiosity was to flourish and expand into a whole new science.

Over the following decades, Edward Thorndike
would investigate whether animals could learn,
and Ivan Pavlov would be awarded the Nobel
prize for demonstrating that reflex responses
could be trained and conditioned. These studies
and others paved the way for the rise in interest in
perception, behaviour and thought.

1881

THE STUDY

RESEARCHER:

Charles Darwin

SUBJECT AREA:

Animal behaviour

CONCLUSION:

Earthworms display
a basic degree of
intelligence.

———————————

ARE WORMS INTELLIGENT?

**DARWIN'S INVESTIGATIONS INTO THE
INTELLIGENCE OF EARTHWORMS**

Worms have no ears or eyes, so how do they function in their environment; is it through learning or instinct?

Charles Darwin was a superb naturalist, and his studies encompassed all sorts of animals, from tiny barnacles to giant tortoises. He was first encouraged to look at earthworms by his uncle Josiah Wedgwood in 1837, and continued to observe their behaviour over the next 40 years in his garden at Down House in Kent. He described his findings in detail in the last book he wrote before his death in 1882: *The Formation of Vegetable Mould through the Action of Worms, with Observations of their Habits*. He called it 'a small book of little moment', but thousands of copies were sold within a few weeks of publication. He was fascinated by the fact that worms bring soil to the surface, thus burying other things, which is why stones sink into the ground. He installed in his garden a worm-stone, which is still there. He went by railway to Stonehenge and drew diagrams showing that some of the great fallen stones had sunk between 10 and 25 centimetres (4 and 10 inches) into the ground.

A family affair

Charles Darwin was a family man and loved being in the garden with his children. He used them as his research assistants, lining them up along the flower beds, and instructing them to note which bees were on which flowers when he blew his whistle. This unusual approach also helped Darwin to gather a lot of data in a short time.

He also enlisted his children to assist with his earthworm studies. He kept a number of worms in flowerpots, and asked his children to try and stimulate them. They tried shining lights on the worms, but having no eyes the worms paid no attention until the lights were extremely bright, and even then only when the light shone on their back ends.

The children blew whistles, shouted at them, and played the bassoon and the piano, but the worms showed no interest. However, if the worms were actually placed on the piano, they reacted immediately when a key was pressed; presumably they could feel the vibration coming through the instrument, even if they could not hear the note.

Instinct or intelligence?

The feature that struck Darwin most forcibly, however, was the apparent intelligence shown by the worms. They had the habit, outside, of pulling leaves into the mouths of their burrows.

> Worms seize leaves and other objects, not only to serve as food, but for plugging up the mouths of their burrows; and this is one of their strongest instincts.
> ... I have seen as many as 17 petioles of a clematis projecting from the mouth of one burrow, and 10 from the mouth of another. Hundreds of such plugged burrows may be seen in many places, especially during the autumnal and early winter months.

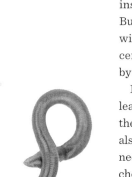

What surprised him most was that they almost always pulled the leaves in by their tips – and since the worms had no eyes, he wondered how they could they find the tips of the leaves. He reasoned that if the worms acted entirely through instinct or chance, they might pull them in randomly. But otherwise they must use intelligence. He pulled 227 withered leaves from worm burrows; 181 of them (80 per cent) had been pulled in by their tips, 20 had been pulled in by the base and 26 by the middle.

He and his son Francis tried cutting the tips off some leaves, and later observed that the worms had instead pulled the majority of them into their burrows by their stalks. They also did various experiments with other leaves and pine needles, and concluded that the worms always seemed to choose the easiest option.

To test his theory further in a controlled experiment, Darwin cut pieces of stiff writing paper into elongated triangles, so that they were similar in shape to leaves. He then used tweezers to pull these triangles into a narrow tube. When they were pulled by the apex – the narrowest corner – they went straight in with the sides curling up to form a neat cone. When they were pulled by a point away from the apex, the task was harder and more of the triangle folded back within the tube.

Next, they rubbed dozens of these paper triangles with fat to prevent them from disintegrating in the dew, and scattered them around his lawn. Over several nights Darwin observed that 62 per cent of the paper triangles that the worms had pulled into their burrows were pulled in by the apex, and the proportion was even higher for narrower triangles.

Darwin and his children carried out hundreds of these experiments, and he came to a firm conclusion:

> *If we consider these several cases, we can hardly escape from the conclusion that worms show some degree of intelligence in their manner of plugging up their burrows.*

CAN YOU LIVE LIFE UPSIDE DOWN?

HOW OUR BRAINS INTERPRET WHAT WE SEE

1896
THE STUDY

RESEARCHER:
George Stratton

SUBJECT AREA:
Perception

CONCLUSION:
Our brains carry out a form of perceptual adaptation that allows us to function when what we 'see' isn't as it seems.

When you look at something, its image is projected on to your retina upside down (as it does on the sensor or film in a camera). In the late nineteenth century, the prevailing scientific theories suggested that this must be necessary if we are to 'see' things the right way up. However, George Stratton, a professor at Berkeley in California, questioned the current thinking, and wondered whether it is possible to live one's life with the whole visual field upside-down. He set about constructing a pair of mini-binoculars that turned everything he saw upside down, so that the image would appear on his retina the right way up, or 'upright', as he put it.

Turning the world over

He placed two convex lenses of equal refractive power in a tube at a distance equal to the sum of their focal lengths. Looking through the tube turned everything upside down.

BELOW: The object you look at casts an upside-down image on your retina. Your brain turns this back the right way up.

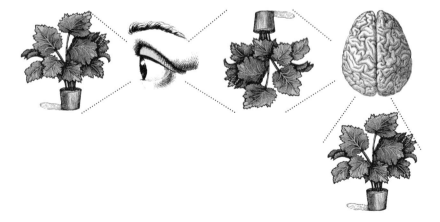

He fitted together two tubes, one for each eye, and strapped the whole contraption to his head. He was careful to exclude all other light, using black cloth and pads round the edges of his device. He wore it continuously for ten hours, then shut his eyes while he removed it, and put on a blindfold so that he could see nothing. He spent the night in complete darkness. The next day he repeated the process, wearing his device all day and taking care not to see anything without it. The instrument gave him a clear field of vision and was reasonably comfortable to wear. At first he hoped to use both eyes together, but coping with two separate images was difficult; so he covered the end of the left tube with black paper, and used his right eye alone.

To begin with everything seemed to be upside down. The room was upside down; his hands, when raised into sight from below, appeared from above. Yet although these images were clear, they did not at first seem real, like the things we see in normal vision, but felt as if they were 'misplaced, false, or illusory images'. Stratton observed that his memories of normal vision still continued to be the 'standard and criterion of reality' that his brain used to understand what was put before his eyes.

Memory or reality

When attempting to move around while wearing the contraption, Stratton at first blundered and stumbled. It was only when his actions were aided by touch or memory – 'as when one moves in the dark' – that he was able to walk or perform hand movements with any degree of success.

Stratton concluded that his problems seemed to consist entirely of the resistance offered by experience, and reasoned that someone whose vision had been upside down from the very beginning (or who had at least spent considerable time observing the world in this way) would not feel that this was unusual. Therefore he carried on this experiment for several days, and, by the seventh day, he reported feeling more at home in the upside-down scene than ever before, recording that there was by now a 'perfect reality in my visual surroundings'.

Getting used to the view

Despite the 'perfect reality' of the upside-down world that he now inhabited, Stratton was still struck by just how difficult it was to operate in such an environment. Having mastered moving in the 'wrong' direction he still found that his perception of depth and distance was flawed: 'my hands frequently moved too far or not far enough. . . .' In trying to shake a friend's hand he raised his own too high, or while brushing a speck from his paper he found he didn't move far enough. And he still observed that his hand movements were much less accurate when he looked at them than when he closed his eyes and depended upon touch and memory to guide him.

Nonetheless, he was, however, gradually getting used to living upside down, and during his walk that evening he was able to enjoy the beauty of the evening scene for the first time since the beginning of the experiment.

Stratton's conclusion was that it does not matter how images appear on your retina; your brain can learn to cope by using what has come to be described as 'perceptual adaptation' to match your vision to your sense of touch and spatial awareness.

ABOVE: The upside-down image maybe disorientating, but your brain can still recognize the setting sun on a summer's evening.

1898

THE STUDY

RESEARCHER:
Edward Thorndike

SUBJECT AREA:
Animal behaviour

CONCLUSION:
There is no evidence
that animals use
reason or memory
to learn.

HOW CLEVER
IS YOUR CAT?

THORNDIKE'S PUZZLE-BOX EXPERIMENTS

At the age of 23, Edward Thorndike wrote one of the first accounts of behavioural research, and laid the foundations for generations of others, notably B F Skinner (see page 37). He took a hungry cat, put it in a box and then placed food outside the box where the cat could see it. The cat could only reach the food by operating some mechanism to open the box. Thorndike made 15 puzzle boxes in all, and labelled them from A through to O. Box A, the simplest, only required the cat to press a lever in order to open the box. In another, the cat had to pull a loop of string to open it and in an even more complex box the cat had to press a lever, pull a string and push down a bar.

Thorndike tried his experiment on several cats, placing them in the same box again and again, and recording how long it took to escape each time. He noted that at first the cats usually tried 'to squeeze through any opening', or to claw or bite their way out of the boxes. He also observed that the cats were not paying very much attention to the food, but seemed to simply 'strive instinctively to escape from confinement'.

However, when the cat was put into the same box again it seemed to become more efficient, 'and gradually . . . after many trials, the cat will, when put in the box, immediately claw the button or loop in a definite way'. In the simplest box one cat took 160 seconds the first time, but after 24 attempts it could escape in 6 seconds. He drew graphs of the time taken to escape against the number of trials, which not only demonstrated that the cats' speed of escape generally improved, but also showed that the more complex boxes

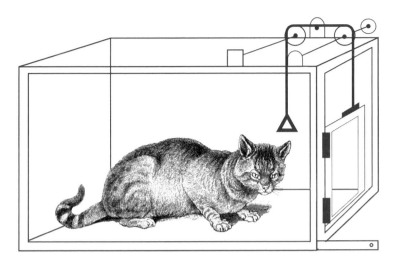

generated more erratic behaviour, and the cats took longer to learn their way out.

He also found that the cats took their learning with them. Cats that had learned to escape from box A by clawing had a greater tendency, when put into another box, 'to claw at things than it instinctively had at the start', and were also less likely to attempt escape by squeeze through holes.

Can cats reason?

Many people in the nineteenth century believed that sophisticated species of animals, such as cats, could learn by association of ideas, and supported this through anecdotes of animals doing apparently clever things. Thorndike was doubtful, writing: 'thousands of cats on thousands of occasions sit helplessly yowling, and no one takes thought of it . . . but let one cat claw at the knob of a door supposedly as a signal to be let out, and straightway this cat becomes the representative of the cat-mind in all the books.'

He also explored whether cats might learn through imitation and let one cat watch another escaping from a box. However, when the second cat was put into the box it went through the same gradual process of learning by trial and error.

Thorndike concluded that there was no real evidence that animals could learn by reasoning. The behaviour of the cats in his boxes was far from reasoned – 'just a mad scramble to get out'. Even when they did manage a successful escape the animals did not seem to remember the technique on their next attempt and still took time trying other things. Furthermore if a cat had learned to escape by pulling a loop, it would continue to claw at the air where the loop had been, even though the loop had been taken away. Thorndike noted that when he reached in and took the cat's paw, put it in the loop and pulled, the cat still failed to learn the trick, and would be clueless next time.

Trials with dogs and chicks

The young scientist also built puzzle boxes for dogs, and pens for chicks. The chicks typically had to step on to a platform, pull a string or peck a tack, but in one of the most complex trials the chick had to climb a spiral staircase, struggle through a hole, walk over a horizontal ladder and jump off a ledge. As with the cats, both dogs and chicks improved with practice, but the chicks learned more slowly than either cats or dogs.

Thorndike wrote in his dissertation: 'when the crude beginnings of this research have been improved and replaced by more ingenious and adroit experimenters, the results ought to be very valuable.' And indeed they were: Thorndike laid the foundations for the new science of behavioural psychology.

DOES THE NAME PAVLOV RING A BELL?

LEARNED RESPONSES AND CLASSICAL CONDITIONING

THE STUDY

RESEARCHER:
Ivan Pavlov

SUBJECT AREA:
Animal behaviour

CONCLUSION:
Conditioning can create powerful responses to otherwise neutral stimuli.

In the late 1890s and early 1900s, the Russian physiologist Ivan Pavlov was leading the field in the exploration of the digestive process. He often used dogs as his subjects and, among his many other observations, he noticed that when their food was delivered by his white-coated assistant, all the animals would begin to drool or salivate.

After many years of study Pavlov knew the body's production of saliva when food, or any foreign body, enters the mouth was a reflex action (an involuntary and often instantaneous response to an external stimulus), which aids digestion or helps to dilute or expel any unwanted matter.

He called this response 'psychic secretion', noting: 'a similar reflex secretion is evoked when [the food and its container] are placed at a distance from the dog and the receptor organs affected are only those of smell and sight. Even the vessel from which the food has been given is sufficient to evoke an alimentary reflex complete in all its details.'

However, he also observed that the dogs soon began to salivate whenever the assistant entered, regardless of whether he brought food: 'the secretion may be provoked even by the sight of the person who brought the vessel, or by the sound of his footsteps.' Pavlov reasoned that the dogs had learned to associate the assistant, or simply just his white coat, with the arrival of food, and so began to salivate in anticipation whenever they saw him.

Pavlov wondered whether he could make the dogs salivate by using a different signal that bore no relation to the food, so he arranged for a metronome to start ticking just before their food was brought in. Sure enough, within

just a few days, he only had to start the metronome and the dogs would salivate, even if no food appeared. He described one experiment in detail:

> *So long as no special stimulus is applied, the salivary glands remain quite inactive. But when the sounds from a beating metronome are allowed to fall upon the ear a salivary secretion begins after nine seconds, and in the course of 45 seconds 11 drops have been secreted. The activity of the salivary gland has thus been called into play by impulses of sound – a stimulus quite alien to food ... The sound of the metronome is the signal for food, and the animal reacts to the signal in the same way as if it were food; no distinction can be observed between the effects produced on the animal by the sounds of the beating metronome and showing real food.*

He tried other stimuli, too: an electric buzzer, the smell of vanillin and probably a bell (although one colleague claimed that Pavlov had never used a bell). He even used an electric shock. In every case the potential stimulus had to be applied a few seconds before the food appeared; if it was applied afterwards, by even one second, then it caused no response.

Natural and conditioned reflexes

Pavlov pointed out that food evokes the salivary reflex in every dog right from birth; this is a natural or unconditioned reflex. Salivation at the sound of the metronome is known as a conditioned response, or a conditioned reflex. He compared this to his newly installed telephone:

> *My residence [is] connected directly with the laboratory by a private line . . . or on the other hand a connection may have to be made through the central exchange. But the result in both cases is the same. The only point of distinction between the methods is that the private line provides a permanent and readily available cable, while the other line necessitates a preliminary central connection being established. . . . We have a similar state of affairs in reflex action.*

Second-order conditioning

Once the dog has begun responding to a conditioned stimulus, a secondary stimulus can be introduced. Thus a metronome is repeatedly started just before food arrives, until the dog salivates at the sound. Then a bell rings with the metronome, and the dog not only salivates, but also associates the bell with food; so when the bell sounds on its own the dog salivates, even though the bell alone has never signalled the arrival of food.

This entire process has come to be called 'classical conditioning', and has been the basis for thousands of subsequent research studies into behaviour and learning, including the controversial case of Little Albert (see page 28).

THE STUDY

RESEARCHER:
Mary Cheves West
Perky

SUBJECT AREA:
Cognition and
perception

CONCLUSION:
When asked to
imagine, our brains
find it difficult to
separate our mental
images from real
perceptions.

CAN YOU IMAGINE A PERKY TOMATO?

COMPARING PERCEPTION, MEMORY AND IMAGINATION

In around 1910, the American psychologist Mary Cheves West Perky carried out a series of ingenious experiments to explore how our imaginations function. First of all she set out to compare real images with mental images, or, as she put it, to compare perceptions with images of imagination.

Her subjects were asked to look at a small ground-glass screen, and told to fixate on the white dot in the centre while imagining a coloured object, such as a tomato or a banana. An unseen projector then began to cast a faint coloured glow on the screen – so faint as to be almost imperceptible – while a tomato-shaped stencil was placed between the projector and screen, so that a very faint image of a red tomato appeared. The edges of the stencil were at first softened with a gauze so that there was no sharp image, and the stencil was moved gently from side to side, to give the appearance of fluttering.

The gauze was gradually removed so that the image became sharper, although it was still exceedingly faint. Meanwhile, the subject explained what he or she was imagining. The red tomato was followed by a blue book, a deep yellow banana, an orange, a green leaf and a pale yellow lemon.

Preparing the set-up was tricky. The primitive projector was hard to use and the two assistants operating it and moving the stencils had to be silent, yet still communicate with the experimenter who sat with the subject. Occasionally things went wrong; a mask slipped, or a shaft of light hit the screen, and the trial had to be abandoned.

Real or imaginary?

All 24 subjects reported imagining the expected images, but none of them reported anything until an image was actually visible (to the researchers) on the screen.

All the subjects were asked whether they were 'quite sure that they had imagined all these things'. They were surprised by the question, sometimes even indignant, and felt certain they had imagined them, saying:

* *I am imagining it all; it's all imagination.*

* *I was making them up in my mind.*

* *The banana is upright; I must have been thinking of it growing.*

Perky's Experimental Set-up

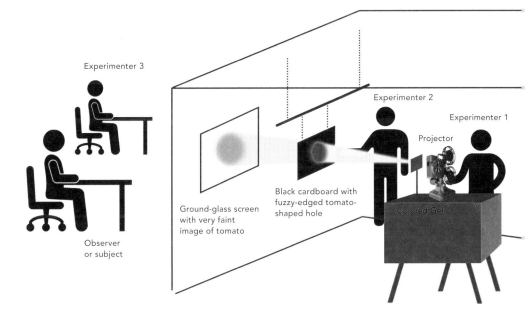

Experimenter 3

Experimenter 2

Experimenter 1

Projector

Black cardboard with fuzzy-edged tomato-shaped hole

Ground-glass screen with very faint image of tomato

Colored Gel

Observer or subject

In fact, many reported some surprise that the banana appeared upright, rather than horizontal as they had first thought of it – yet this seemed to arouse no suspicion. One graduate student even supplied additional context: he saw the tomato painted on a tin; the book was a particular book whose title he could read; the lemon was lying on a table.

This experiment indicated that people find it extremely difficult to distinguish between perception and imagination – between seeing something and imagining it. This is known as the Perky Effect, and remains true today.

Images from imagination and images from memory

In her next series of experiments Perky tried to distinguish between mental images created from imagination and those influenced by memory. She had noticed that when she tried to create a mental picture of something personal, such as her own bedroom or home, she had to reach into her memory, and she tended to move her eyes about when thinking, as if searching for the object. Whereas when she imagined something impersonal, such as a tree or a boat, it had to come from the imagination and she didn't move her eyes. Her brain appeared to operating in a different way to carry out the different tasks.

To test this today, psychologists would use laser eye-trackers, but lasers had not been invented in 1910; so Perky had to invent another way to look for eye movement.

The subjects sat in a dark room and were asked to envisage something personal or something impersonal. They were instructed to keep their eyes on a bright spot on the wall in front of them while they did so. There were several other bright spots just outside their field of view. Out of 426 trials, images from memory appeared in 212, and in 90 per cent of these the subjects reported seeing extra bright spots, showing that they must have moved their eyes.

Images from imagination appeared in 214, of which 68 per cent showed no eye movement. Eye movements here seemed to be caused by images of animals running across the scene, or by vistas too wide to be seen without eye movement. Occasionally the subjects would 'see themselves' in the image: 'there was somebody in the boat which I supposed was myself.'

Perky also found that sound images caused movement of the larynx when the image was from memory, but not when it was from imagination, while memory smell images produced movements of the nostrils.

Perky wrote: 'the mood of memory is that of familiarity or recognition, intrinsically pleasant, the mood of imagination is that of unfamiliarity or novelty.' She concluded that memory involves eye movement and some body movement, while imagination requires steady fixation, but no movement. Also memory images are scrappy, filmy and give no after-images, while images of imagination are substantial, complete and sometimes give after-images.

CHAPTER 2: The challenge of behaviourism: 1920-1940

After the work of Thorndike and Pavlov became widely known, psychologists became more interested in the study of behaviour, both in humans and other animals. All sorts of remarkable experiments were carried out that shaped the science of psychology (although some, such as John B Watson's classical conditioning of baby Albert, would be considered cruel by today's standards). B F Skinner, arguably the

most famous behaviourial psychologist of all, devised ingenious tests for rats and pigeons, to discover how they learn. In Berlin, 'Gestalt' psychologists tried to understand the human ability to make meaningful perceptions in a chaotic world, and in the United States, scientists marched into the factory looking for new ways to improve efficiency and productivity. The psychology of business had begun.

1920

THE STUDY

RESEARCHERS:
John B Watson and
Rosalie Rayner

SUBJECT AREA:
Behaviour

CONCLUSION:
All individual
differences in
behaviour are due to
different experiences
of learning and
conditioning.

WHAT'S THE MATTER WITH LITTLE ALBERT?

EXPLORING CLASSICAL CONDITIONING IN HUMANS

Albert B, or 'Little Albert' as he came to be known, was a placid, happy, healthy child, who weighed 9.5 kilograms at the age of nine months, and had lived almost all his life in a hospital, where his mother was a wet nurse.

In 1919, psychologist John B Watson and his graduate student, Rosalie Rayner, set out to test whether a human would respond to the same kind of conditioning that Pavlov had carried out with his dogs (see page 19). Watson hypothesized that a baby's fear of loud noises is, like a dog's salivation, an innate, reflex response. He reasoned therefore, that, through the principles of classical conditioning, it should be possible to provoke fear in response to otherwise unrelated objects.

Watson and Rayner chose Little Albert as their subject and began by first presenting him with a live white rat, then a rabbit, a dog and a monkey, as well as a range of other objects. He seemed to want to handle them, but showed no fear at this stage and didn't cry.

Next, they made a loud and surprising noise by hitting a steel bar with a hammer just behind his head. Their notes report:

The child started violently, his breathing was checked and the arms were raised in a characteristic manner. On the second stimulation the same thing occurred, and in addition the lips began to pucker and tremble. On the third stimulation the child broke into a sudden crying fit. This is the first time an emotional situation in the laboratory has produced any fear or even crying in Albert.

Classical conditioning

Then they set out to test whether they could condition fear of an animal, specifically a white rat, by visually presenting it and simultaneously striking a steel bar, and then whether this conditioned fear would be transferred to another animal. Establishing conditional emotional responses as follows:

> *1. White rat suddenly taken from the basket and presented to Albert. He began to reach for rat with left hand. Just as his hand touched the animal the bar was struck immediately behind his head. The infant jumped violently and fell forward, burying his face in the mattress. He did not cry, however.*
> *2. Just as the right hand touched the rat the bar was again struck. Again the infant jumped violently, fell forward and began to whimper.*

They showed him the rat and walloped the iron bar three more times. By this time Albert had begun to whimper when he saw the rat alone. Then they gave him two more treatments with rat and noise, and finally, as soon as the rat was shown alone 'the baby began to cry. Almost instantly he ... began to crawl away so rapidly that he was caught with difficulty before reaching the edge of the table.' Thus the unconditioned response to the noise had become a conditioned response to the rat.

A few days later, knowing that Albert was still afraid of the rat but otherwise appearing happy and smiling, Watson and Rayner wanted to see if his fear of the rat would be transferred to other furry animals and began by showing him the rabbit. He leaned as far away from the animal as possible and then burst into tears. He was less upset at the sight of the dog, but still began to cry, and was also disturbed by cotton balls.

Researchers continued to condition the child with the rat and the dog, hammering the steel bar as soon as they came close to him. A month after these experiences Albert continued to show signs of distress in response to the rat and the dog, and was still uncomfortable with the rabbit.

Questionable ethics

This experiment was considered highly controversial at the time and has since been heavily criticized both for the validity of its findings and its morality. This sort of experiment would never be allowed today, and there is some doubt about whether Albert's mother actually gave formal consent at the time. Watson himself made small note of the questionable ethics behind his venture: 'at first there was considerable hesitation upon our part in making the attempt . . . A certain responsibility attaches to such a procedure.' But quickly he took 'comfort' from the notion that 'such attachments would arise anyway as soon as the child left the sheltered environment of the nursery for the rough and tumble of the home'.

Watson also recorded that he had wanted to try 'detachment' or desensitization – the removal of the conditioned emotional responses – but Albert was taken away from the hospital before this could be attempted.

There is no evidence that the conditioning lasted (and no evidence that it remained), since efforts to find Albert were made only recently. The most likely candidate seems to have been one Albert Barger, who died in 1987 before anyone had contacted him.

His niece said he had always disliked dogs.

DO YOU WORRY ABOUT UNFINISHED BUSINESS?

THE ZEIGARNIK EFFECT

1927

THE STUDY

RESEARCHER:
Bluma Zeigarnik

SUBJECT AREA:
Cognition and
memory

CONCLUSION:
Incomplete tasks
or events without
'closure' are more
easily remembered
(or less easily
forgotten) than those
that are completed.

Bluma Zeigarnik was a Lithuanian psychologist working at the Berlin School of experimental psychology in the 1920s. Professor Kurt Lewin roused her curiosity when he observed that a waiter could remember all the orders that had not been paid for, but once they were paid for he promptly forgot them.

Zeigarnik set out to investigate. She gave 164 individual subjects 22 simple tasks, such as writing down the names of cities beginning with L, making clay models or building boxes out of cardboard. During half of the tasks Zeigarnik interrupted the subjects before they had time to complete them. Afterwards she found that subjects remembered 68 per cent of the unfinished tasks but only 43 per cent of the finished ones.

Some subjects were interrupted when a task was almost finished; these people recalled 90 per cent of the unfinished tasks. Our ability to remember unfinished tasks in much greater detail than those we satisfactorily completed, as well as our desire to see it completed, has come to be called the 'Zeigarnik effect' and it occurs in many areas of our lives. For example, 200 students questioned after an exam were found to remember many more of the questions they had been unable to answer than those they had answered correctly.

It is evident that we can worry about unfinished business for days, just because it is unfinished. This is why producers of soap operas for television and radio so often conclude each episode with a cliff-hanger; it keeps the audience thinking about the problem until the next programme.

One interesting possible consequence of the Zeigarnik effect is that students whose learning is interrupted to do unrelated things – sport or socializing – may actually remember their work better than those who never stop studying; perhaps all work and no play really does make Jack a dull boy. It should be noted, however, that this does not apply to those who interrupt themselves before anything has actually been learned.

The frustration of interruption

Interrupting a task also influences the subject's estimate of how long the task takes, as was shown by a study in 1992. Subjects were asked to unscramble ten three-letter anagrams: GBU, TEP, ARN, FGO, OLG, UNF, TAS, TOL, EAC, UNP. Then they were asked to estimate how much time it had taken. Their guesses proved to be within 10 per cent of the actual time.

Next the subjects were asked to solve 20 three-word anagrams – EDB, ANC, YDA, ODR, OTE, UME, ADL, XFO, DLI, XEA, PZI, AEG, ARO, BTI, SYE, NIF, GRA, FTI, DCO, ILE.

Halfway through the task they were asked to estimate how long the task had taken so far. Their estimate was 65 per cent longer than the actual time. Then they completed the task and again asked to estimate how long the second half had taken. This time their estimate was 35 per cent higher than the real time.

Their first estimate seems to have been so high because they were frustrated at being interrupted, and felt a sense of failure, which appears to have made them think they were slower than they really were.

Can closure help?

Zeigarnik herself concluded that we naturally feel the need to complete tasks, following the Gestalt notion of 'closure'. The finished task is a completed Gestalt, and we can stop thinking about it. Failure to complete the task sets up tension which is not resolved until the original need is satisfied. Zeigarnik wrote:

> *The strength with which such tension systems arise and persist evidently varies greatly between different individuals but remains very nearly constant with the same individual. Strong needs, impatience to gratify them, a child-like and natural approach – the more there is of these, the more will unfinished tasks enjoy in memory a special advantage over those which have been completed.*

Furthermore, according to John Gottman, in his 2013 book *What Makes Love Last?*, arguments between lovers that are resolved by confession or discussion do much less harm than denial, or regrettable incidents that go unaddressed, for then the pain persists in active memory and becomes a constant and dangerous irritant. It seems humans seek completion, or 'closure' in many areas of their lives.

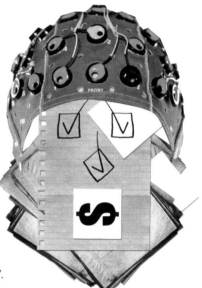

Contradicted by cash?

However, a study at the University of Mississippi in 2006 showed that the Zeigarnik Effect can be undermined when money changes hands. Forty college students were asked to carry out a five-minute task while they would be measured for 'hemispheric-activity'. They were fitted with fake recording apparatus – a plastic helmet fitted with electronic chips and wires leading to a computer – and left to begin the task. Half the students had been promised $1.50 for taking part; but the other half expected no reward. Halfway through the alloted time the students were informed that the 'hemispheric recording' was complete. Forty-two per cent of the students receiving payment immediately abandoned the task. Of the volunteer half, only 14 per cent left before the task was complete.

1932

THE STUDY

RESEARCHER:

Frederic Bartlett

SUBJECT AREA:

Cognition and
memory

CONCLUSION:

Remembering is
not simply the recall
of static facts, but
an active process,
similar in kind to
imagining and thinking.

ARE YOU GOOD AT TELLING TALES?

THE ACCURACY OF LONG-TERM MEMORY

As part of his long investigation into how memory works, Frederic Bartlett, the first Professor of Experimental Psychology at the University of Cambridge, tested people's ability to remember figures, photographs and stories. He persuaded his subjects to read and retell various short stories; one of his favourites was the following Canadian folk tale.

'The War of the Ghosts'

One night two young men from Egulac went down the river to hunt seals, and while they were there it became foggy and calm. Then they heard war cries and they thought: 'maybe this is a war party.' They escaped to the shore and hid behind a log. Now canoes came up and they heard the noise of paddles and saw one canoe coming up to them. There were five men in the canoe and they said: 'what do you think? We wish to take you along. We are going up the river to make war on the people.' One of the young men said 'I have no arrows.' 'Arrows are in the canoe,' they said. 'I will not go along. I might be killed. My relatives do not know where I have gone. But you,' he said, turning to the other, 'may go with them.' So one of the young men went but the other returned home. And the warriors went on up the river to a town on the other side of Kalama. The people came down to the water, and they began to fight, and many were killed. But presently the young man heard one of the warriors say: 'quick, let us go

home; that Indian has been hit.' Now he thought:
'oh, they are ghosts.' He did not feel sick but they
said he had been shot. So the canoes went back to
Egulac and the young man went ashore to his house
and made a fire. And he told everybody and said:
'behold I accompanied the ghosts and we went to
fight. Many of our fellows were killed and many of
those who attacked us were killed. They said I was
hit and I did not feel sick.' He told it all and then
he became quiet. When the sun rose he fell down.
Something black came out of his mouth. His face
became contorted. The people jumped up and cried.
He was dead.

Less-than-total recall

Bartlett asked his first subject to read the story, and then tell it from memory to a second subject, who in turn told it from memory to a third, and so on until they reached seven reproductions. The effect was similar to the children's game 'Telephone', in which a message is passed from person to person, gradually mutating on the way, as people introduced errors or changes.

Not surprisingly the story changed and lost details as it was told and retold. The subjects were all young British men, not familiar with the style and content of the story, and they made many mistakes. In particular they steadily shortened the story and left out details. On the other hand the story became more coherent – Bartlett called this 'conventionalization' – and it remained a sensible story. The tale became more British, as the subjects inserted words and ideas from their own cultural backgrounds. For example some of the subjects remembered 'hunting seals' as 'fishing', and 'canoes' as 'boats'. They also forgot and excluded elements that did not make sense to them.

Another of Bartlett's methods was to ask one subject to read the story, retell it and then retell it again after various

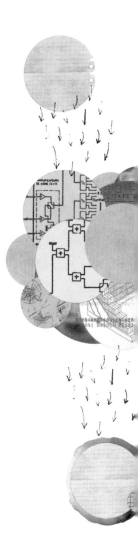

STORY

SCHEMA

MODIFIED STORY

periods of time – perhaps half an hour, a week or three months. This method achieved similar results.

Using schemas

Bartlett suggested that long-term memory consisted of 'schemas', where each schema was 'a mass of organized experiences', or 'an active organization of past reactions, or past experiences'. He believed that 'the past operates as an organized mass rather than as a group of elements each of which retains its specific character.' He concluded that all new incoming information interacts with the old information in the schema, to make a modified schema. Remembering, he suggested, is not a process of picking static facts from a rack, but an active process, not fundamentally different from imagining and thinking. Recalling a memory is therefore a process not of reproduction, but of reconstruction, within what may well be a new cultural context, and constitutes 'an effort after meaning'. In remembering something like the 'War of the Ghosts', because the story must inevitably be reinterpreted in the light of the general character of the subjects' previous experience.

Bartlett used tennis as an analogy for his findings. He said that with each stroke of the racket, he did not produce something absolutely new, and he never merely repeated something old. The stroke was literally manufactured out of the living visual and postural schemas of the moment, and their interrelations.

Bartlett's schema approach was not widely accepted at the time, but has come into favour more recently, and in particular was championed by computer scientist Marvin Minsky in the field of artificial intelligence.

HOW DO
ANIMALS LEARN?

'OPERANT CONDITIONING' AND
REINFORCEMENT OF BEHAVIOUR

1938
THE STUDY
RESEARCHER:
Burrhus Frederic
Skinner
SUBJECT AREA:
Animal behaviour
CONCLUSION:
Positive reinforcement
is more effective
than punishment in
shaping behaviour.

After the pioneering work of Thorndike (see page 16) and
Pavlov (see page 19), the American psychologist B F Skinner
took a more scientific approach to animal learning. He
thought there was no point in trying to understand what
an animal wanted or planned; he preferred to see what it
actually did in tests carried out under controlled laboratory
conditions. He observed that humans appear to learn from
the consequences of their actions, and that we repeat actions
that are rewarded, such as working hard at school. Skinner
wondered if animals learn in the same way, and whether by
studying animals he might be able to uncover fundamental
principles of how people learn.

Operant conditioning
Skinner put a rat in a box that contained a lever. When the rat
pressed the lever a food pellet was dispensed. To begin with
the rat just ran around the box, but when by chance it pressed
the lever it noticed the arrival of the food. This was positive
reinforcement in its most direct form. Quite soon the rat
learned that whenever it pressed the lever it got food, and it
began to press the lever five times a minute.

Skinner described only what he could observe, and never
stated that the rats learned to press a lever because they
wanted food. He explained that it was the action, not the
rat, that was reinforced (or sometimes punished). He called
this process operant conditioning, because the rat learned
not from any stimulus but from its own actions. Skinner's
'operant conditioning' differs from the classical conditioning

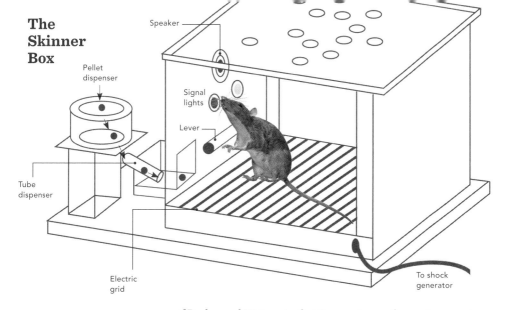

The Skinner Box

Speaker

Pellet dispenser

Signal lights

Lever

Tube dispenser

Electric grid

To shock generator

of Pavlov and Watson in that it operates on the environment, rather than on the reflexive behaviour of the subject.

'Chaining'

Skinner boxes were similar to Thorndike's puzzle boxes, but often more elaborate, and linked to automatic recording devices; he knew exactly how often the rat pressed a lever without having to sit there with a notebook.

In another box, food was dispensed only after a lever was pressed ten times, but the rats soon learned to do this, and indeed afterwards they pressed their lever more often than those in an 'every-time' box.

Gradually he made his boxes more elaborate, with more difficult things for the rats to do. In some cases he used unpleasant stimuli; as the rat wandered around its box it might suddenly be bombarded by loud noise, but when it accidentally touched a lever, the noise was turned off. In due course it learned to press the lever as soon as it was put into the box. In another box, rats would learn to press a lever as soon as a light came on, because otherwise they would receive an electric shock shortly afterwards.

Skinner found that rats could learn to perform a complex sequence of simple actions, as long as they learned them one at a time. A rat could learn, for instance, to turn when a buzzer sounded, and then press a lever after a light came on; food would be dispensed. Skinner called this process 'chaining.'

Using pigeons in place of rats
Skinner also ran trials with pigeons and found that they could learn to peck at a red spot on the wall for a food pellet to appear. Indeed it would peck even if food appeared sometimes, rather than every time. Skinner pointed out that this was just like a gambler with a one-armed bandit. The gambler has learned that putting a coin into the machine and pulling the lever will occasionally yield a reward; he or she just hopes it will be big enough to compensate for the investment.

Skinner found that pigeons, like rats, could learn to perform complex tasks, such as turning in a circle and then pecking at a target, as long as there was reinforcement for each step. As Skinner himself said, 'The consequences of behaviour determine the probability that the behaviour will occur again.' He was convinced that by using his principles it should be possible to create a Utopian society, where all behaviour would be good, and everyone would be happy. In his novel *Walden Two* (1948), he describes a wonderful community where people worked only four hours a day, benefited from superb recreation, were environmentally responsible and enjoyed complete equality between the sexes.

RESEARCHERS:

Fritz Jules
Roethlisberger and
W. J. Dickson

SUBJECT AREA:

Social psychology

CONCLUSION:

Paying attention
to the thoughts
and feelings of
workers will
increase productivity.

CAN PSYCHOLOGY INCREASE PRODUCTIVITY?

THE HAWTHORNE EFFECT

The Hawthorne Works, at Cicero, Illinois, was an enormous factory built by Western Electric in 1905. In 1924 their electrical suppliers claimed that better lighting would increase productivity and the managers at Hawthorne commissioned a study to find out whether this was true.

The researchers measured productivity, divided the workforce into a test group and a control group, and then carefully increased the light levels for the test group. To the surprise of the investigators, productivity shot up in both groups. Then they made the test group's workplace progressively dimmer, and, until they began to complain that they could not see what they were doing, the productivity of both groups rose again. Productivity even went up when they returned the light levels to where they had been in the first place. Intrigued, the researchers tried changing the work environment in various other ways.

The longest-running study focused on the assembly of electrical relays – switching devices used in telephone exchanges. Making a relay required repetitive work, putting together by hand 35 pins, springs, armatures, insulators, coils and screws. Western Electric produced over 7 million relays a year, and the speed of individual workers determined overall production levels.

The relay test room

The experimenters chose two women and invited them to choose four more to make a team, and set them up in a separate test room. Here an experimenter discussed changes with them, and at times implemented their suggestions. The experimenters wondered whether the women might get tired during their long working days, and therefore slow down. So they suggested the possibility of two five-minute rest periods during the day; after some discussion the women chose to have them at 10 a.m. and at 2 p.m. They appreciated the breaks, but some commented that they were too short.

When the experimenters discovered that the productivity had gone up, they offered ten-minute breaks instead. Some of the women were worried that they would not be able to make up for the time lost, but the experimenters suggested that they would work faster because they would be less tired. The women loved their longer breaks and they actually produced more relays than ever before. When the researchers changed to six five-minute breaks, however, productivity went down.

The researchers tried serving lunch during a 15-minute break in the morning. They shortened the working day by half an hour, and output increased; they shortened it again: output per hour increased, but daily output dropped. Then they put the working day back to where it had been originally, and output reached the highest level ever, up 30 per cent.

The final set of tests was to introduce an incentive pay scheme with 14 men in the Bank Wiring factory. The surprising result was that productivity did not increase; the men in the group had established a 'norm' for themselves, and kept working at the same rate, in spite of the offer of more pay for more work.

The experimenters noted that almost everything they did – apart from offering more money – produced a temporary increase in productivity.

Conclusion

One conclusion was that productivity depends on informal interactions in the work group. In addition, this group had an interested and sympathetic supervisor who provided feedback on their efforts. Another possibility was that the workers wanted to please the experimenters, which is often the case in psychological experiments.

Hawthorne superintendent George Pennock said that:

> ... a relationship of confidence and friendliness has been established with these girls to such an extent that practically no supervision is required. In the absence of any drive or urge whatsoever they can be depended upon to do their best. They say they have no sensation of working faster now than under the previous conditions. They have a feeling that their increased production is in some way related to the distinctly freer, happier and more pleasant working environment.

The Hawthorne studies showed that productivity will increase if the management treat the workers with respect and as human beings, rather than as mere appendages to the machines they operate. These ideas were entirely new in the 1930s, but the Hawthorne experience made it clear that organizations that do not pay attention to personal and cultural values will be less successful than those that do.

HOW DO YOU MANAGE A DEMOCRACY?

EXPLORATIONS IN LEADERSHIP STYLES AND GOOD GOVERNANCE

1939

THE STUDY

RESEARCHERS:
K Lewin, R Lippitt,
and R K White

SUBJECT AREA:
Social psychology

CONCLUSION:
Effective democracy
needs proactive
group management
rather than unlimited
individual freedom.

After the pioneering psychologist Kurt Lewin escaped Nazi Germany in 1933 and fled to America, he wrote about:

> *... the peculiar mixture of desperate hope, curiosity, and scepticism with which the newly arrived refugee from Fascist Europe looks at the United States. People are fighting for it, people are dying for it. It is the most precious possession we have. Or is it but a word to fool the people? Democracy?*

How could he learn what a real democracy was like, and how to organize it? First, he set up a 'lab' that was really more like a kids' den – a space in an attic, with wooden boxes to sit on, surrounded by all sorts of junk – mainly construction equipment – and enclosed by crude sacking walls. It was crowded, undisciplined, unstructured and fun – just the opposite of a clean white classroom.

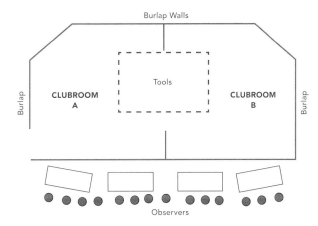

He recruited groups of 10- and 11-year-old children, and divided them into four clubs, each of which would meet once a week. The children were asked, with the help of an adult leader (who was one of the researchers) to make theatrical masks, make furniture and paint signs for the room, carve soap and wood, and build model aircraft. In other words their club room was also their workshop.

Lewin deliberately aimed to set up different types of social climate by using different styles of leadership – groups of children would experience first one type of leader and then another, over several weeks. A dozen researchers sat in a dark corner and took notes of how the children were reacting to one another, and to the leader, while Lewin himself secretly filmed the proceedings. Interestingly, this was one of the first experiments in social psychology in which the experimenters played central parts, as leaders; before this they had merely been the observers or helpers.

Three styles of leadership

The first leader was strict; he told the children exactly what to do, step by step, so that they rarely knew what the final plan was. He told them which child should do which tasks, and exactly where they should work – mostly in the centre of the floor. In his praise or criticism he was direct and personal. He always stood in one place, wore a suit and tie and remained outside the group.

The second leader set up a 'democratic atmosphere' in which the entire club discussed the project in advance, and took decisions about what to do. They chose their own working groups. When they asked for advice, the leader suggested two or three options for them to choose from. He was entirely objective in his praise and criticism of their performance. He was one of the group: took off his jacket, rolled up his sleeves and moved around the space with the children, although he did little actual construction.

The third leader just sat still, let the children get on with it, and scarcely interfered at all. This 'laissez-faire' attitude happened originally by mistake, when a new leader, Ralph White, forgot to steer the children towards democracy, and anarchy set in. As he said later: 'the group started to fall apart. There were a couple of kids who were realhell-raisers, and they found a great opportunity to raise hell, which wasn't productive.'

The results

In the first regime there was endless trouble. The strict leadership led to a great deal of tension; arguments and fights broke out between the children. They were clearly unhappy, and tended to blame one another for mistakes. After one session they smashed up the masks they had been making. As Lippitt noted, 'They couldn't fight the leader, but they could [fight] the masks.'

In the democratic atmosphere the children were much happier, less aggressive and more objective about the work. They were also much more productive and imaginative, doing their work all over the club room.

In the laissez-faire groups, the children rarely concentrated on their tasks, but just wandered around the room. The researchers decided that this style of leadership was also interesting; so they persisted, and the leaders had to work hard at being passive and uninvolved.

When children were moved from one group to another they rapidly shifted to the new regime, and learned how to fit in with the group and the leader.

Lewin concluded that democracy would never come from unlimited individual freedom; it would need strong, proactive group management. The experiment showed that democratic behaviour can be generated in a small group, which ushered in the concept of focus groups and group therapy. More important, it showed that leadership should be a teachable skill, and need not merely be associated with charisma or military prowess.

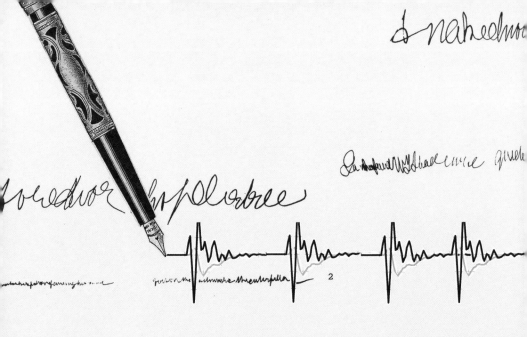

CHAPTER 3: **Changing concerns: 1941–1961**

After World War II, psychologists widened their focus from human and animal behaviour to include the practical ramifications of studying the mind. Questions arose about how psychology could help in the classroom, and researchers devised ways of studying how children think. Scientists examined whether animals could solve problems, and pondered what those answers meant in terms of human interaction. Pure 'thinking' was not the only subject matter: emotional and social behaviour became relevant

realms of psychology. In these contexts, new questions arose. How do you track emotions as fundamental as a mother's love for her baby? Can we believe in two totally disparate or contradictory realities? Why is conformity so important to us? And is aggression an innate trait?

1948
THE STUDY

RESEARCHER:
Edward C Tolman

SUBJECT AREA:
Animal behaviour

CONCLUSION:
Rats displayed latent learning and can memorize details, demonstrating cognitive behaviours.

CAN RATS MAKE MENTAL MAPS?

HIDDEN, LATENT OR INCIDENTAL LEARNING

The famous behaviourist B F Skinner (see page 37) had said that it was not worth considering what animals might think about or want; all you could do was see how they reacted to reinforcement. Berkeley professor Edward Tolman was not so sure. He wanted to find out how much they can think, and what they hold in their memories.

Like Skinner, Tolman and his students built mazes for rats to run through, but they specifically designed mazes that would show thinking – cognitive behaviour – by the rats. One of the first of these was a series of narrow passages connected by T-junctions on a horizontal surface (the plan is shown at the top of page 50).

The rats were divided into three groups. Once a day each hungry rat was put in at the bottom left of the maze and had to find its way to the top right. On the way it came to six T-junctions, and had to choose the correct turn each time; so it had six possibilities for going wrong.

Rats in group 1 always found a food pellet at the end of the maze. The result was that they learned their way through the maze more quickly each day, and by the seventh day were making no wrong turns at all, as you can see in the graph opposite. (The graphs show the average for each groups of rats.)

Delayed reward

For six days the rats in group 2 found no food at the end; so there was no incentive for them to hurry. They wandered about, making various wrong turns each day, but at the end of the seventh day they found the food, which was there on all subsequent days. On the eighth day they made only one wrong turn, and on the ninth day they went directly to the food with no errors. Group 3 found food at the end of the third day, and afterwards found their way to it rapidly.

The point here is that the first group took seven days to work out the direct route to the food. The second and third groups took only two or three days to do it, once they knew the food was waiting. It follows that in their earlier wanderings, they must have formed a mental map (or 'cognitive map') of the maze, even though there was no hurry to get to the end. This was hidden learning, since the fact that they had formed a mental map was not obvious until after they found the food and their learning was not revealed until then. It is also called 'latent learning', or 'incidental learning'.

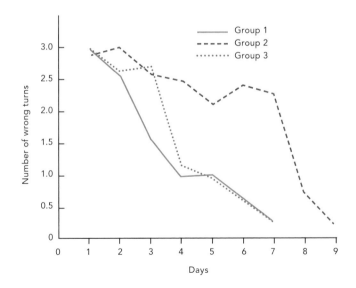

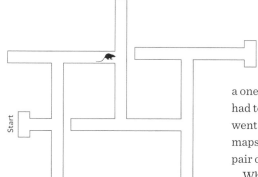

Start

Food

Maze with six T-junctions

Two-dimensional maps

Tolman pointed out that solving this task needed only a 'strip map' – that is a one-dimensional map. Essentially the rats only had to learn 'right' or 'left' for each junction. He went on to investigate whether the rats can form maps in two dimensions, and built a more complex pair of mazes.

When he replaced the simple maze with a far more complex one that offered the rats a choice of directions, most of the rats chose precisely the right path to get to where the food had been before. In other words they had not just learned 'left, right, right, left . . .', but had worked out the direction relative to their starting position, or to the room they were in.

An even more elegant experiment, which Tolman reported regretfully had been carried out by others (Spence and Lippitt), used a simple Y-shaped maze, as shown below, with food at the end of the left arm and water at the end of the right. Rats were placed at the base of the Y, but because these rats had just had access to food and water they did not eat or drink in the maze. For the crucial test the animals were then divided into two groups. One group was made hungry (but not thirsty); the other group thirsty (but not hungry). When put into the maze each rat from the hungry group went straight to the food; those from the thirsty group went straight to the water. This shows that they must have made and retained a mental map of the maze, even when they were neither hungry nor thirsty.

So next time you find yourself working out the best route from your bedroom to the front door, or from the supermarket to the train station, remember that rats – and other animals – may use mental maps just like us.

F

W

The Y-shaped maze

S

WHAT ARE YOU THINKING, CHILD?

PIAGET'S THEORY OF COGNITIVE DEVELOPMENT IN CHILDREN

1952
THE STUDY

RESEARCHER:
Jean Piaget

SUBJECT AREA:
Developmental
psychology

CONCLUSION:
Children think
differently to adults
and their learning
gradually develops in
measurable stages.

Jean Piaget was a Swiss psychologist who, after interviewing boys at a school, began to wonder how children think. Most people imagined that children were just like adults, but less good at thinking. He showed they are born with a primitive mental structure which they gradually develop with learning, and that they think in ways that are quite different from adults.

He developed his theories by talking to children, including his own, and by doing experiments to tease out aspects of their thoughts about the world.

Conservation

Young children, he found, don't understand the concept of conservation. He showed them two identical wide glasses containing the same amount of liquid. Then he poured the liquid from one of the glasses into a tall narrow one, so that the liquid there was deeper. Almost without exception, children aged two to seven said there is now more liquid in the thin glass.

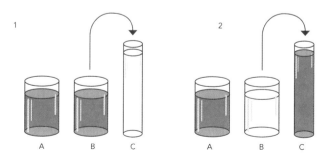

Piaget's
Conservation
Task

Children were fooled when he placed two lines of sweets on the table, with equal numbers in each line, but with the sweets close together in one, and further apart in the other. When he asked them which line has more sweets he noted:

Children between 2 years, 6 months old and 3 years, 2 months old correctly discriminate the relative number of objects in two rows; between 3 years, 2 months and 4 years, 6 months they indicate a longer row ... to have 'more'; then after 4 years, 6 months they again discriminate correctly.

Piaget defined four stages of development: 'sensory-motor' from zero to two years, 'pre-operational' from two to seven years, and so on. In the first part of the second stage, from two to four years, children begin to use symbols to represent their world. They will draw their families, and although the drawings are not to scale or even remotely like the people, the children don't seem to mind.

In the second part, from about four to seven, children become curious and ask enormous numbers of questions, some of which show signs of reasoning. Some are impossible to answer: I remember my son asking 'Why is it a cat?' And while I was wondering what to say, he followed it up with 'And what happens if it isn't?'

Piaget suggested that children develop 'schemas' – building blocks of intelligent behaviour, or actual units of knowledge (see page 36). Even tiny babies have a few schemas, including a sucking schema; they will suck nipples, comforters or fingers. These schemas are constantly being revised and added to as the child investigates the world, and, as children develop and grow, they develop more schemas to include the new information they acquire. When new information can go straight into an existing schema it is assimilated; when it won't fit then it has to be accommodated by modifying an existing schema into something larger.

Egocentric views?

Small children, he surmised, have an egocentric view of the world, which means they cannot imagine things from someone else's viewpoint. He demonstrated this with a neat experiment, called 'The Mountain Scene.'

The child was shown a three-dimensional model of three different mountains; one had a cross on it, and one had a tree. A teddy bear or doll was seated on the other side of the table. The child was then shown a series of pictures, and asked which one showed the scene from the doll's point of view. Invariably they chose the one that showed their own view, rather than the doll's.

Piaget wrote: 'far from representing the various scenes which the doll contemplates from different viewpoints, the child always considers his own perspective as absolute and thus attributes it to the doll without suspecting this confusion.'

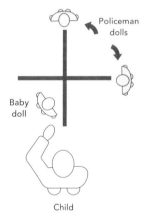

This experiment has been criticized on the grounds that the children may not have understood the question and similar studies with less complex set-ups have achieved different results. For example, in 1975 the British developmental psychologist Martin Hughes showed children a model of two intersecting walls, with two model policemen and a model baby. He asked the children to put the baby where he would be hidden from both policemen. The children were aged from 3.5 to 5, and 90 per cent of them gave correct answers, even though they needed to understand the points of view of both policemen.

Piaget's work remains influential in both developmental psychology and education, though his developmental stages have been subject to many subsequent revisions.

1953

THE STUDY

RESEARCHERS:
Morris F. Heller and
Moe Bergman

SUBJECT AREA:
Neuropsychology

CONCLUSION:
Subaudible
tinnitus may be
a phenomenon
experienced by
everyone without
their knowledge.

WHAT'S THAT NOISE?

IS TINNITUS AN ILLNESS, OR IS IT ALL IN OUR HEADS?

Some people suffer from a ceaseless buzzing or ringing in their ears; it stops them from hearing; it interrupts their sleep; and it can make their lives a misery. This buzzing or ringing is called tinnitus and the sensation can vary from faintly irritating to downright unpleasant.

Before the 1950s it was suggested that there were two types of tinnitus. Vibratory tinnitus, caused by real sounds from a physical source such as muscle activity and non-vibratory tinnitus – an illusion of sound caused by an irritation of the auditory neural elements; that is, it came from inside the brain.

Doctors have suggested all sorts of possible treatments for the condition, including medication with half a dozen different types of drugs; elimination of all drugs and intoxicants; correction of faulty gastrointestinal function or blood-forming organs; dietary control of fluids, salt and water balance; dental work; medication inside the ear; psychotherapy; or the use of a hearing aid – not to mention a variety of surgical operations.

Is tinnitus an illness or a symptom?

One researcher, E P Fowler, who had once asserted that tinnitus is always associated with deafness, altered his view and noted that it was often present in people who had no apparent ear disease. He went on to examine 2,000 patients, and found tinnitus in 86 per cent of them.

Morris F Heller and Moe Bergman, two American doctors specializing in audiology, noted that tinnitus at times appeared to interfere with their patients hearing, but

they wondered if, actually, the reverse were true. Perhaps the symptom of tinnitus became more apparent as the patients' hearing worsened:

> Patients often state that were it not for their head noises, their hearing would be better, and that when the head noises are louder the deafness is more severe. It does not necessarily follow that the tinnitus is always responsible for this. Possibly with increased deafness the head noises are less easily masked and so appear louder subjectively.

Loudness is measured in decibels (dB); very loud noises, such as drills or motorbikes, produce 100 dB, while normal conversation is about 70 dB and whispering about 50 dB. Heller and Bergman estimated that the loudness of tinnitus was only around 5 to 10 dB above the threshold of human hearing – the quietest sound one could hear.

Heller and Bergman wondered, since tinnitus had been observed in perfectly healthy people, whether it may be an early symptom preceding impaired hearing. And they realized that they could study subaudible tinnitus (tinnitus that people cannot normally hear) by exposing healthy people to an extremely quiet environment.

The soundproof room

Heller and Bergman recruited 80 volunteers from a variety of backgrounds (all healthy adults, aged from 18 to 60) who had normal hearing, and reported no deafness or tinnitus.

Each person was taken into a soundproof chamber, where the ambient noise level was probably between 15 and 18 dB (they could not measure it precisely because the sound-level meters at the time were not sophisticated enough).

The volunteers sat in the soundproof chamber for five minutes and were asked to make notes of any sounds they heard; there was no suggestion that the source of the sound might come from within the subject's head. The researchers also tested 100 hard-of-hearing patients.

The results were surprising. Of the hard-of-hearing patients 73 per cent reported hearing sounds. Of the other, hearing subjects, 94 per cent reported hearing sounds. In all they reported 39 different sounds. Most people reported hearing one sound; some reported two and a small fraction reported three, four or five. These results suggest that the effect of tinnitus is present for almost everyone, but is normally masked by the ambient noise that floods the environment. In ordinary quiet living conditions the ambient noise is usually more than 35 dB, which seems to be loud enough to hide the tinnitus, which remains subaudible.

Incurable condition

One immediate conclusion drawn from Heller and Bergman's research is that tinnitus cannot be 'cured' by treatment, and at best can only become subaudible. Yet this has not prevented many people from continuing to suggest causes, preventive measures and cures.

THE END IS NIGH, OR IS IT?

THE DISCOMFORT OF COGNITIVE DISSONANCE

1956

THE STUDY

RESEARCHERS:
Leon Festinger, Henry Riecken and Stanley Schachter

SUBJECT AREA:
Cognitive dissonance

CONCLUSION:
Humans find coping with two or more contradictory beliefs highly distressing.

In August 1954, Marian Keech predicted that the world would end in a great flood, just before dawn, on 21 December. Mrs Keech was the leader of a semi-religious cult called The Seekers. She claimed to receive messages by 'automatic writing', where her hand and the pen seemed to function all by themselves, and words appeared in handwriting quite unlike her own. These messages ranged from descriptions of the environment on other planets, to warnings of war and devastation on Earth, along with promises of amazing joy and salvation for all true believers. She claimed to have had received the apocalyptic message from the planet Clarion, and added that just before the flood a flying saucer would come to carry The Seekers away to safety.

The believers

The other members of the group – a doctor, his wife and other middle-aged professionals – quit their jobs, left their husbands and wives, and gave away their money and possessions to get ready for the trip. As one put it, 'I've given up just about everything. I've cut every tie; I've burnt every bridge. I've turned my back on the world. I can't afford to doubt. I have to believe.'

Leon Festinger and his colleagues saw the headline in a local newspaper – PROPHECY FROM PLANET CLARION. CALL TO CITY: FLEE THAT FLOOD – and decided to infiltrate the group and follow the action. As social scientists

they wanted to observe what psychological processes would happen when the prophecy failed. In October they went to visit Mrs Keech, and managed to join the cult.

Occasionally they got into difficulties; one evening Mrs Keech invited researcher Hank Riecken to lead the evening session. He was terrified: if he refused, he would arouse suspicion, but if he agreed, he might put his foot in it and ruin everything; so he agreed, and then as the session began, he raised his hand and said, 'Let us meditate.'

As the fateful day approached, the researchers noted that the group avoided publicity, gave interviews grudgingly and allowed only true believers into Keech's house.

Preparing for lift-off

On 20 December the group expected a 'Guardian' from outer space to call on them at midnight and take them to a waiting spacecraft. In the evening they carefully removed all metal objects, including coins, rings, buttons, zippers, belt buckles and bra straps. At 12:10 a.m. there was still no visitor and the group was reduced to horrified silence. At 4 a.m. Mrs Keech began to cry.

At 4:45 a.m. another message came to Keech by automatic writing. It said that the little group, sitting all night long, had spread so much light that the God of Earth had decided to save the world from ultimate destruction.

Suppose you were a member of the group; what would you do now? Would you replace all those metal things, leave quietly, sneak back home and hope that your family and your boss would take you back without too much fuss? One member did just that, but the rest of The Seekers did exactly the opposite.

Resolving the conflict

Changing tack completely, they began an urgent campaign to spread their message to as wide an audience as they could. By 6:30 they had phoned newspapers and arranged interviews, trying to bring the whole world into their belief system. They searched outer space for guidance, made various other prophecies and began to issue pamphlets detailing them. In other words, far from driving them away, the events actually increased their allegiance to the cult.

Festinger said that for this remarkable turnaround, they must have held their beliefs with deep conviction, must have taken important action that could not be undone, must have understood that the prediction had gone completely wrong and must have had firm support from the others in the group.

He said they had changed their stance because of the mental stress caused by holding two incompatible beliefs at the same time. He called this 'cognitive dissonance.' We come across it all the time. Suppose your friend Bob has bought a new car, or a new phone. He will probably say it is the best, fastest, most efficient, most economical and so on. This may all be true, but what is more important is that he has invested time and money in making the purchase, and does not want you or anyone else to suggest it is not altogether perfect.

In the case of The Seekers, Festinger suggested that once the world had not ended, and they were faced with severe cognitive dissonance, the believers found it easier to modify the original prophecy, and to accept the additional belief that the aliens had actually saved the world because of their efforts rather than accept that the prophecy (and therefore their deeply held beliefs) was flawed.

1956

THE STUDY

RESEARCHER:
Solomon E Asch

SUBJECT AREA:
Social psychology

CONCLUSION:
A percentage of
subjects will agree
with a group decision,
even if they believe it
to be wrong.

WOULD YOU BUCKLE UNDER PEER PRESSURE?

ASCH'S EXPERIMENTS IN CONFORMITY

Would you always say what you believe to be true, even if several other people say you are wrong?

Groups of individuals often seem to take group decisions: 'let's all go to the restaurant', or 'we'll all sing "Happy birthday to you."' Sometimes, however, one or two will disagree, and decide to do something else. Behavioural psychologist Solomon Asch wanted to measure how much people are persuaded by the rest of the group.

The experiment

A male college student was invited to join a group of other students for a psychological study. He found them waiting in a passage, and they all went into a classroom, where the new recruit found himself sitting last but one in the row of six or seven others. What he did not know was that they were all stooges, and had been given a strict set of rules to follow. He was the only outsider – the 'critical subject'.

An experimenter came in and explained that what they had to do was estimate the relative lengths of lines. For each trial he put on a stand a card with three black lines of different lengths, and a separate card with one test line, which was the same length as one of the three. The lines varied from 2.5 to 25 centimetres (1 to 10 inches) long. The job of the team was to say which line was the same length as the test line.

Here was the important part: they had to call out their choice aloud, one by one; so the critical subject was the second last to speak, and had already heard several answers before it was his turn. Each experiment had 18 trials, which in fact consisted of nine trials repeated twice.

All the stooges always gave identical answers; so if the first said it was line B all the others said the same. For the first two trials everyone gave the right answers. In the third trial the stooges deliberately chose the wrong line, and the critical subject, often looking puzzled, had to choose whether to say what he thought was the right answer, or to go along with the majority. This was a tough decision, for he had to speak out in public, and to disagree meant that he was saying that all the others were wrong.

Then they carried on with the subsequent trials; the stooges gave right answers in six of the 18 trials, and wrong answers in 12 of them. Curiously, the critical subjects succumbed, and gave wrong answers, most often in trials four and ten, which involved the same set of lines.

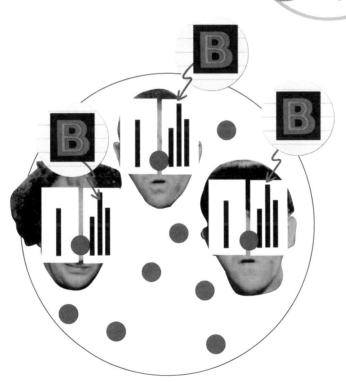

To make sure that choosing the correct line was reasonably easy, Asch ran a series of trials in which a single subject looked at the sets of lines, and wrote down his answers. Without peer pressure, the subjects were accurate more than 99 per cent of the time; so the task was not too difficult.

Asch went through dozens of these experiments, and the overall result was that the critical subjects went along with the majority and gave 'wrong' answers in 37 per cent of the trials. Some critical subjects remained completely independent, and ignored all the others in the group. Others gave in completely, and simply went with the majority every time. Some chose a middle ground, and in 20 per cent of the trials gave wrong answers that were not as wildly wrong as those of the majority, but still wrong.

He interviewed them all after the trials, and found that they tried to explain why they had been confused:

- *I thought they were measuring width after a while.*

- *I thought there was some trick to it – an optical illusion.*

- *First I thought something was the matter with me or most of them.*

- *I was sure they were wrong, but not sure I was right.*

The pressure of the group

Later in each interview Asch revealed what had been going on; the victims were all greatly relieved. One even went so far as to say, 'The duty of a government is to do the will of the majority, even if you are convinced they are wrong.' Others gladly shared their relief:

- *Either these guys were crazy or I was – I hadn't made up my mind which – I was wondering if my judgements really were as poor as they seemed to be, but at the same time I had the feeling that I was seeing them right.*

- *I agreed less because they were right than because I wanted to agree with them. I think it takes a lot of nerve to go in opposition to them.*

- *When I disagreed I felt outside the group.*

Asch came to a series of conclusions. With only two or three stooges the critical subjects were more likely to be independent, and less swayed by the majority. The pressure of the majority did not build up with time; most of the critical subjects maintained a constant level of independence. So peer pressure really works, although these experiments were only about judging the length of lines; more research would be needed to find out how far it goes. But in general, as one victim put it, 'It is hard to be in the minority.'

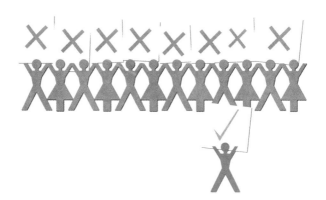

RESEARCHERS:
H F Harlow and
R R Zimmermann

SUBJECT AREA:
Developmental
psychology

CONCLUSION:
Evidence suggests
that maternal
attachment is based
on more than feeding.

HOW DO BABIES FORM ATTACHMENTS?

MATERNAL SEPARATION, DEPENDENCY NEEDS AND SOCIAL ISOLATION

Why do babies form strong attachments to their mothers? Is it a natural automatic process, or is it something they learn because their mothers feed them? The controversial American psychologist Harry F Harlow wrote:

> *Psychologists, sociologists and anthropologists commonly hold that the infant's love is learned through the association of the mother's face, body, and other physical characteristics with the alleviation of internal biological tensions, particularly hunger and thirst. Traditional psychoanalysts have tended to emphasize the role of attaching and sucking at the breast as the basis for affectional development.*

In other words, either the baby goes to its mother for milk, and learns to associate the food with her face, smell and feel, and so becomes conditioned to attach to her, or there is an innate evolutionary bond ready to be formed, regardless of the supply of milk. Harlow wanted to find out which of these is right by exploring the effects of mother and infant separation. Realizing that using human babies was impossible, he turned to the rhesus macaque monkeys held at his workplace in the University of Wisconsin Primate Laboratory.

He had to find a way to separate the supply of milk from the warmth and softness of the mother. He noticed that after they had been taken from their mothers, the babies spent some time clinging to their cloth nappies, and this gave him an idea.

Surrogate mothers

He took eight baby monkeys from their mothers between six and 12 hours after birth, and put each one in a cage with two surrogate mothers made of stiff wire mesh, fitted with crude heads. One mother was wrapped in terry toweling cloth, the other was left bare.

In four of the cages the wire mother was equipped with a feeding bottle that dispensed milk; the terry-cloth mother had no milk. In the other four cages only the terry-cloth mother had milk. Both sets of monkeys drank the same amount of milk and put on the same amount of weight, but the critical observation was that in all eight cages the infants spent most of their time climbing and clinging on to their terry-cloth mothers.

The baby monkeys were left with these surrogate mothers for six months. Generally those whose milk came from the wire mother went briefly to her when they were hungry or thirsty, but spent most of the time with the terry-cloth mother, and formed an affectionate bond with her – a bond that was strong and stable.

The fact that they spent so much time with their soft mothers was evidence that the attachment is not just about food, but something more instinctive. Harlow wondered, however, whether the terry-cloth mothers would provide comfort and security when the babies were frightened. So he presented them with a mechanical bear with a drum that made a loud noise. Regardless of which mother had provided milk, the terrified babies all cuddled up to the terry-cloth mum. This echoes the behaviour of baby monkeys raised by their real mothers. The babies spend many hours every day clinging to their mothers, and run to them for comfort and reassurance when they are frightened.

'Open-field test'

He put each baby in novel environments with strange objects, and found that if their surrogate mothers were there, they would cling to her for a while, then go off and explore, and run back to her when they got scared. If she was not there they would just curl up in a corner and stay there, sucking their thumbs.

Human babies who are deprived of affection often have difficulty forming emotional ties later in life. Harlow found similar behaviour in his baby monkeys. He took four babies from their mothers and left them without even surrogate mothers to bond with. After eight months he put them into cages with both cloth and wire surrogate mothers, but they failed to form attachments to either surrogate. Harlow concluded that baby monkeys develop normally only if they can cling to a cuddly object during their first few months; clinging seems to be a natural, automatic response to stress.

On the other hand they seemed to need social rather than maternal interaction. Another group of four babies were brought up on their own, but every day they were put into a cage for 20 minutes with the other three. These monkeys grew up with relatively normal emotional and social behaviour.

Harlow's work casts some light on the behaviour of human babies (it suggests, for example, that prolonged bodily contact with the mother is beneficial), but it has been heavily criticized as unnecessarily cruel. His babies never became entirely normal; when placed in a cage with a monkey that had been brought up by its mother the 'orphan' would huddle miserably in a corner, and always show signs of unhappiness. He also created much anxiety in the mothers that were deprived of their babies; they often became neurotic, and attacked their babies furiously if they were reintroduced.

HOW SHORT IS SHORT-TERM MEMORY LOSS?

THE FAST DECAY OF ICONIC MEMORY

THE STUDY

RESEARCHER:
George Sperling

SUBJECT AREA:
Cognition and memory

CONCLUSION:
Human possess a powerful short-term visual memory.

If you saw a row of random letters, such as **N D R K S Q**, how many could you remember? And what if you saw a whole grid of letters? George Sperling, an American psychologist working at the famous Bell Laboratories in New Jersey, wanted to find out how much can be seen in a brief exposure, and how long can we remember it. We normally see the world in brief glimpses between eye movements called 'saccades'; so presumably we must get our whole world view in brief glimpses. Sperling set up a simple and elegant set of experiments to investigate.

One problem was finding a way to show images so briefly. He used a tachistoscope, which allowed him to show a card to the subject for a fraction of a second; the two-field mirror tachistoscope was considered state-of-the-art equipment in 1960.

From 55 centimetres (22 inches) away the subjects were shown 12 x 20 centimetres (5 x 8 inches) cards, each with an array of half-inch-high letters. The tachistoscope was generally set to give a flash of light lasting 50 ms (one twentieth of a second). There were 500 different cards so no one learned any of the letter patterns, except for a few striking ones, such as **XXX**.

Some cards had three, four, five, six or seven letters in a line, either normally spaced or bunched together. Others had two or three rows of letters, either spaced or bunched. No vowels were used.

R N F B T S

K L B J
Y N X P

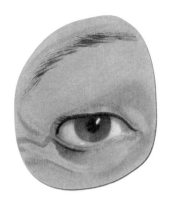

Experiment 1

The subject saw one of these arrays for 50 ms, and then had to write down the letters in the correct places on a grid. They were told to guess any they were not sure about. In each run the subjects saw between five and 20 cards, at a pace of their own choosing – generally about three or four per minute. All the subjects could consistently score 100 per cent when there were only three letters.

When there were more letters, the subject's scores (immediate-memory spans) varied, but remained almost constant for each subject, ranging from 3.8 to 5.2. The average immediate-memory span was about 4.3 letters. The arrangement of the letters, whether bunched or spaced, and whether in one row or more, did not make much difference.

Experiment 2

Sperling then tried varying the length of the flash, exposing the card for periods from 15 ms up to 500 ms (half a second). Surprisingly, this made no appreciable difference to the scores; the limit stayed the same.

Experiment 3

Sperling noticed that the subjects often said that they had seen more than they could remember afterwards, which seemed very odd. Do we really see things and then forget them so quickly? He realized that this meant that the question 'What did you see?' asked them to report both what they could remember and what they had forgotten.

He devised a brilliant procedure to find out whether they had really seen more than they could say. He actually showed them far more information than they could possibly report, but asked them to report only some of it.

This time the subjects saw two rows of letters, with either three or four letters in each row. They were told that immediately after the light had gone off, a tone would sound for half a second. If it was a low tone they had to report the lower row; if it was a high tone they had to write down the upper row. Later they saw three rows, and three tones.

high tone	**D W R M**
medium tone	**S K Z T**
low tone	**Q M C R**

The results were astonishing. The subjects scored a higher percentage of correct letters than they had before, and their accuracy increased day by day with practice; after seeing cards with 12 letters, their average score reached 76 per cent. In other words they must have 'seen' about nine of the 12 letters.

This suggests that at the time of the exposure, and for a few tenths of a second afterwards, the subjects had two or three times as much information available as they could later report. Sperling writes 'the persistence is that of a rapidly fading, visual image of the stimulus.'

This graph shows the number of letters available. The numbers of letters on the card are shown along the bottom axis. The maximum score is the diagonal line. The lower curve shows the immediate memory (experiment 1); the upper curve shows the number of letters available, as revealed by experiment 3.

Average all subjects

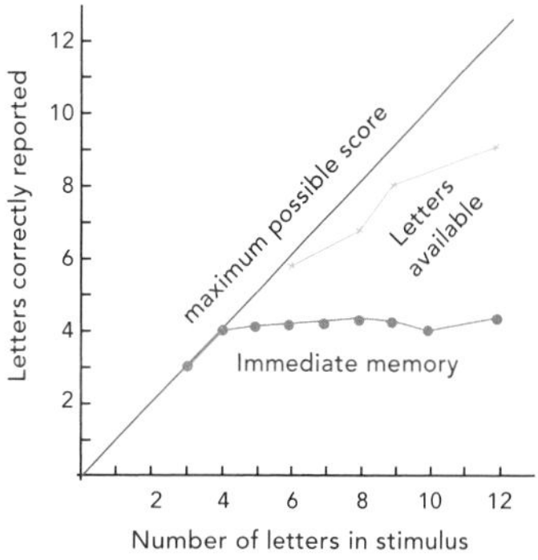

Letters correctly reported (y-axis: 2, 4, 6, 8, 10, 12)

maximum possible score

Letters available

Immediate memory

Number of letters in stimulus (x-axis: 2, 4, 6, 8, 10, 12)

Iconic memory
Shown a white card immediately after the card with letters, the subjects did much worse, suggesting overload of the visual system, and supporting the idea that the letters must have been held as a persisting visual image.

In other words, Sperling had discovered a quickly forgotten, picture-like memory. Nobody had ever suggested such a thing before. Today it is called 'iconic memory', or visual short-term memory (VSTM).

1961

THE STUDY

RESEARCHERS:
A Bandura, D Ross,
and S A Ross

SUBJECT AREA:
Developmental and
social psychology

CONCLUSION:
Children exposed to
aggressive behaviour
are more likely to
act in physically
aggressive ways.

IS AGGRESSIVE BEHAVIOUR LEARNED?

THE BOBO DOLL EXPERIMENT

Children are bombarded by aggressive behaviour on television and in electronic games. By the age of 10 or 11, most children will have seen thousands of murders and hundreds of thousands of acts of violence, all of which tends to be glamorized. Even cartoon characters get swatted, flattened or thrown off cliffs. Does this endless violence encourage kids to be violent?

That is what Albert Bandura and his colleagues wanted to find out. So they took three groups of children aged between three and six, exposed one group to aggressive behaviour by adult role models, one group to normal behaviour and left the control group alone; and then watched to see what the children would do. The researchers expected that girls would be more likely to imitate a female role model, and boys a man. They also expected boys to be more aggressive, especially after watching an aggressive male role model.

The experiment

Each child was taken into a room, and the role model was then invited to come in and join the game. The child sat in one corner with a table, and material to make pictures using potato prints and stickers. The role model went to the opposite corner, where there was a small table and chair, a Tinkertoy set, a mallet and a 1.5 metre (5 feet) Bobo doll – a life-size inflated character that always bounces up again when pushed over.

In half the trials the models were not aggressive, they sat and assembled the Tinkertoys, ignoring the Bobo doll.

In aggressive trials the models worked on the Tinkertoys for a minute, and then spent the rest of the time violently attacking the Bobo doll: punching it, sitting on it and punching it repeatedly on the nose, lifting it up and bashing it on the head with the mallet, then tossing it up in the air and kicking it furiously around the room. They then repeated these actions about three times, shouting 'SOCK HIM IN THE NOSE ... HIT HIM DOWN ... THROW HIM IN THE AIR ... KICK HIM ... POW.'

Ten minutes later the female experimenter came back, and took the child to another building. After two minutes' play in an anteroom they went into the observation room, where she waited, but sat in a corner keeping busy with paperwork at a desk, and avoiding any interaction with the child.

In this experimental room was a variety of toys, from crayons and paper, a ball, dolls, bears, cars and lorries, to plastic farm animals; but also a mallet and a 1 metre (3 feet) inflated Bobo doll. Each child spent 20 minutes in this room, while their behaviour was rated by judges, watching through a one-way mirror.

After they had watched the non-aggressive model, the boys were almost invariably more aggressive than the girls, especially with the mallet, and the Bobo doll. Whether the role model had been male or female did not seem to make an enormous amount of difference, and the amount of aggression was much the same as was shown by girls and boys in the control group, who had not witnessed the actions of the role models, although both girls and boys in

the latter group were decidedly vicious with the mallet. An interesting feature was that both boys and girls who had watched a non-aggressive man showed less aggressive behaviour than those who had not watched anyone.

There were much greater changes in the children who had witnessed aggressive behaviour. Girls turned out to be considerably more aggressive than boys in their shouting, after seeing a female role model shouting, while boys shouted more after seeing the man shouting.

The Bobo doll

Curiously, in punching the Bobo doll the boys were more aggressive after watching a woman doing it, but the girls were more aggressive after watching a man.

In almost every category the children who had watched aggressive behaviour were noticeably more aggressive than those who had not, which confirmed the researchers' predictions that violent behaviour would be learned. They concluded that in masculine type behaviour such as physical aggression, both boys and girls imitate a man more than a woman. On the other hand for verbal aggression ('HIT HIM DOWN . . . THROW HIM IN THE AIR . . . KICK HIM . . . POW') both boys and girls imitated the model of their own sex more than the other.

There were noticeable sex differences in the children's comments about the aggressive models: 'who is that lady? That's not the way for a lady to behave. . . . She was just acting like a man. I never saw a girl act like that before. She was punching and fighting.' And on the other hand, from a girl 'That man is a strong fighter, he punched and punched and he could hit Bobo right down to the floor. . . . He's a good fighter, like Daddy.'

These experiments have been quoted thousands of times, and yet still the argument goes on: does seeing violence on the screen make children violent?

DO YOU WANNA BE IN MY GANG?

GROUP MENTALITY AND THE GANGS OF ROBBERS CAVE

1961
THE STUDY
RESEARCHERS:
M Sherif, O J Harvey,
B J White, W. R.
Hood, and
C. W. Sherif
SUBJECT AREA:
Social psychology/
conflict theory
CONCLUSION:
Conflict arises from
competition for
resources rather than
individual differences.

What is it about groups or gangs that creates tension, and what can be done to prevent it? All over the world there are problems when rival groups compete for scarce resources. People complain bitterly about immigration, because they think that foreigners will take their jobs. Inner-city gangs compete over drugs and territory. Competition over land, or water, or oil, frequently escalates into war and even genocide.

Social psychologist Muzafer Sherif, born and educated in Turkey, was interested in Realistic Conflict Theory. He decided to set up deliberate conflict between groups, and then see how it could be resolved.

Robbers Cave

He invited two groups of 12-year-old boys to a summer camp at the Robbers Cave State Park in Oklahoma. The 11 white middle-class boys in each group did not know one another; nor did they know about the other group. For the first week both groups went swimming and hiking, and did baseball practice together, and so established their own cultures. One group called itself the Eagles; the other group the Rattlers, and they stencilled the names on their T-shirts and flags.

Next, the researchers arranged for the groups to compete over several days at baseball, tug-of-war, touch football, tent pitching and a treasure hunt, and promised prizes to the winners – a trophy for the team and a medal and a four-bladed knife for each member – but nothing to the losers, in order to provoke frustration. When they first heard of

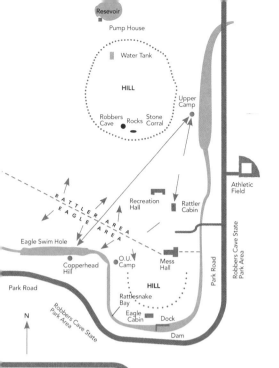

General layout of the campsite and respective areas of the two camps

these competitions, the Rattlers were totally confident they would win. The competition was level until the final event, the treasure hunt, which the researchers rigged so that the Eagles won. They were 'jubilant at their victory, jumping up and down, hugging each other, making sure in loud tones that everyone present was aware of their victory. On the other hand, the Rattlers were glum, dejected and remained silently seated on the ground.' One group went for a picnic, but were delayed on the way, and when they arrived found that the others had eaten all their food.

The friction increased. The groups started name calling and taunting each other. The Eagles burnt the Rattlers' flag; the Rattlers ransacked the Eagles' cabin. Both groups became so heated that the researchers had to physically keep them apart.

Sherif noted that:

> *The derogatory attitudes toward one another are not the consequence of preexisting feelings or attitudes. ... They are not the consequence of ethnic, religious, educational or other background differentiation among the subjects. The state of friction was produced systematically through the introduction of conditions of rivalry and frustration perceived by the subjects as stemming from the other group.*

They then spent two days cooling down, but Sherif found, as he expected, that bringing the groups together was not enough; they kept calling one another names, and at meals they threw food and napkins at one another. The best way to resolve the conflict, he decided, was to present the groups with a problem too large for either to solve alone – Sherif called it a 'superordinate goal' – so that they had to work together.

The researchers cut off the water supply at the tank above the camp, then announced that to sort it out would need about 25 people. Members of both groups volunteered. By the time they reached the tank they were thirsty, but could get no water. At this stage they began to cooperate to remove the sacking that had been blocking the pipe (put there by the experimenters).

The next task was over money. The boys were told they could see a film, but it would cost $15 to get it from town, and the camp could afford only $5. After much discussion and voting, both groups agreed to contribute, and they all enjoyed the film. Later both groups went by lorry to camp at Cedar Lake, where they were induced to work together to tow a lorry which was 'stuck', and then both groups agreed to cook food for everyone, on alternate days.

Finally, they all went home on the same bus, and even agreed at a rest stop on the way that the $5 prize one group had won should be spent on buying drinks for everyone.

Nearing Oklahoma City, the boys at the front of the bus (mostly high status members from both groups) began to sing 'Oklahoma.' Everyone in both groups took part, all sitting or standing as close together as possible in the front end of the bus. A few boys exchanged addresses, and many told their best friends that they would meet again.

Conclusions

Sherif believed that because the groups were created to be approximately equal, individual differences are not necessary for intergroup conflict to occur. When the boys were competing for valued prizes, hostile and aggressive attitudes arose because they were competing for limited resources.

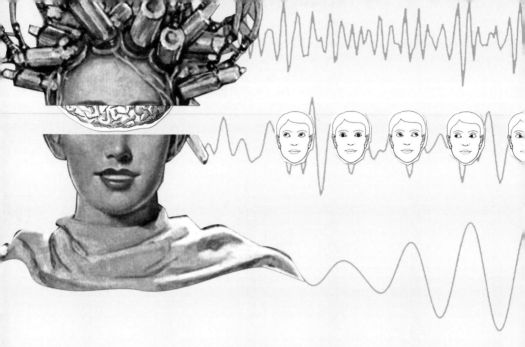

CHAPTER 4: Mind, brain and other people: 1962-1970

By the mid-60s, psychology was flourishing. The field was becoming a 'respectable' science, and noted courses were opening in both universities and secondary schools worldwide. The growing numbers of psychologists and experimenters explored a widening range of topics – such as how bystanders react to emergencies or the invasion of personal space. The interest in social psychology and human behaviour in group situations blossomed, especially after Milgram's

influential studies into obedience and subordination to authority. In addition, the 1960s also saw the beginnings of new technology, such as the invention of electroencephalography (EEG), which enabled the first looks inside the living brain. As technology advanced, so did the opportunities to combine neuroscience and psychology, leading to a wealth of new directions for the field.

RESEARCHER:

Stanley Milgram

SUBJECT AREA:

Social psychology

CONCLUSION:

Some subjects will obey an authority figure who instructs them to act against their conscience.

HOW FAR WOULD YOU GO?

THE MILGRAM EXPERIMENT

Yale psychology professor Stanley Milgram wanted to find out how far volunteers would go in obeying authority. He was prompted by C P Snow's 1961 comment that 'more hideous crimes have been committed in the name of obedience than have ever been committed in the name of rebellion.' He was also painfully aware that before and during World War II millions of innocent people were slaughtered on command, in the gas chambers of death camps.

'Teachers' and 'learners'

Milgram invited 40 volunteers to take part in a learning experiment, ostensibly to test the effect of punishment on memory. Each volunteer met another person in the lab at Yale University; the procedure was explained to them by an impassive, stern-looking experimenter in a grey lab coat, and they were invited to draw slips of paper from a hat to find out which of them would be 'teacher' and which would be 'learner.' In practice this was rigged; all the slips of paper were marked 'teacher'; so the volunteer was always the 'teacher.'

The 'teacher' then saw the 'learner' being strapped into a chair and an electrode attached to his wrist. If the 'teacher' queried this, the experimenter explained that 'Although the shocks can be painful, they cause no permanent damage.'

The 'teacher' was then taken to another room, and was able to communicate with the 'learner' only by sound, using a microphone and headphones.

For the memory test, the 'teacher' read out a list of word pairs. Then he repeated the first word, and four possibilities

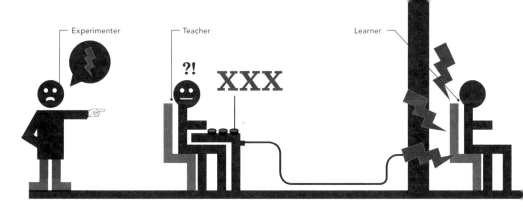

for its pair. If the 'learner' got it right the 'teacher' moved on to the next word in the list. If it was wrong, he was to administer an electric shock, by pressing a switch. There were 30 switches in a line, and the teacher was to start at the beginning and move up one switch at each wrong answer.

How far would they go?
The first shock was only 15 volts ('Slight shock'), but they went up to higher and higher voltages – 30 volts, 45 volts, 60 volts and so on up to 420 volts ('Danger: severe shock') and a maximum of 450 volts (simply marked 'XXX'). As each switch was pressed, a pilot light was illuminated in bright red; an electric buzzer sounded; an electric blue light labelled 'voltage energizer' flashed; and the voltage meter swung to the right.

In order to convince the 'teacher' of the authenticity of the generator before the experiment began, he was given a 45-volt sample shock.

In fact the 'learner' was a trained confederate of Milgram's – a 47-year-old accountant – and the 'shock generator' was a dummy; he received no real shocks. The 'learner' kept answering questions, often wrongly, up to 300 volts; after that he did not speak at all. What the 'teacher' heard instead was pounding on the wall between them.

At this point the 'teacher' usually asked the experimenter for guidance, and was told to wait ten seconds for an answer, and then deliver the next higher shock. After 315 volts he again heard pounding on the wall, but from this point there was no further response to increasing shocks.

At some point the 'teacher' usually asked whether he should go on with the test. The experimenter replied with a series of prods, delivered politely but firmly:

1. Please go on.
2. The experiment requires that you continue.
3. It is absolutely essential that you continue.
4. You have no other choice; you must go on.

How many 'teachers' do you think would refuse to carry on the sadistic procedure? You might imagine that most of them would quickly have refused to go on, and a group of psychologists predicted that at the very worst three per cent of the volunteers would go right through the sequence. In fact none of the 'teachers' stopped below 300 volts, and no fewer than 26 carried right on to the final 450 volt shock.

As each experiment proceeded, all the 'teachers' sweated profusely, trembled, stuttered, groaned, dug their fingernails into their palms and 14 of them broke into nervous laughter. At some point a few of them did actually refuse to carry on.

Responsibility?

The ramifications of this astonishing series of experiments are profound. In the twenty-first century prison guards from the Nazi death camps are still being hunted down and tried for war crimes, but were they just obeying orders? Groups of soldiers of many nationalities have been accused of hideous atrocities – including raping and murdering innocent civilians – but were they just obeying instructions from superior officers? And if so, does this relieve them of responsibility for their actions?

CAN YOU EVER RECOVER FROM BLINDNESS?

LEARNING TO SEE AT THE AGE OF 50

1963
THE STUDY

RESEARCHERS:
R L Gregory and
J G Wallace

SUBJECT AREA:
Cognition and
perception

CONCLUSION:
Sensory experience is
not straightforward.

What would it be like to recover your sight after being blind for 50 years? Born in 1906, S B lost the sight of both eyes at the age of ten months after a smallpox vaccination. At the Birmingham Blind School in England he turned out to be bright, and good at mental arithmetic; he learned to recognize capital letters by feeling plastic ones. He was ambitious, and became adept at carpentry, knitting and boot repairing. When he left school he got a job repairing boots at home.

As R L Gregory later discovered, 'He was proud of his independence as a blind man. . . . He would go for long cycle rides, holding the shoulder of a friend, and he was fond of gardening, and making things in his garden shed.'

Seeing again

To clear his vision he had surgery in December 1958 and in January 1959. When the bandages were removed, the first thing he saw was the surgeon's face. He heard a voice coming from in front of him and to one side: he turned to the source of the sound, and 'I saw a dark shape with a bump sticking out and heard a voice, so I felt my nose and guessed the bump was a nose. Then I knew if this was a nose, I was seeing a face.'

The surgeon reported that:

> *After the operation he . . . could recognize faces and ordinary objects (i.e., chairs, bed, table, etc.) immediately. His explanation is that . . . he had a*

definite and accurate mental image of all things he was
able to touch.

Gregory and Wallace first saw S B seven weeks after the first operation. He 'struck us immediately as a cheerful, rather extrovert and confident, middle-aged individual.... He could even tell the time by means of a large clock on the wall. We were so surprised at this that we did not at first believe that he could have been in any sense blind before the operation. However, he proceeded to show us a large hunter watch with no glass, and he demonstrated his ability to tell the time very quickly and accurately by touching the hands.'

Three days after the operation he saw the moon for the first time. When he was told it was the moon, he expressed surprise at its crescent shape, expecting a 'quarter moon' to look like a quarter piece of cake.

Illusions that failed

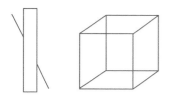

Gregory showed him some well-known illusions, including the Poggendorf Illusion and reversing depth illusions: most people say the diagonal line is not straight, but S B simply said 'All one line.'

Do the Necker cube and the steps to the left look three-dimensional? Can you get them to flip inside out, from one perspective to the other? Can you see the steps from underneath? For most people the Necker cube and the steps will turn 'inside out' as you look at them – the steps can be seen either from above or from below – but S B saw no depth, and the figures did not reverse. Asked to draw pictures, S B was at first slow and incompetent, but gradually improved. On the left are three of his drawings of a bus, done 48 days, six months and one year after the first operation.

One of the features Gregory and Wallace found intriguing was how S B transferred information from early touch experience to vision many years later. He could recognize capital letters that he had learned by touch, but could not recognize lower case letters that he had not learned by touch.

In the Science Museum in London, he was fascinated by the Maudslay screw-cutting lathe. From outside the glass case he could not 'see' it, but when the case was removed and he was allowed to touch it, 'He ran his hands eagerly over the lathe, with his eyes tight shut. Then he stood back a little and opened his eyes and said: "now that I've felt it I can see." He then named many of the parts correctly and explained how they would work.'

In his book *Dioptrics* (1637), René Descartes wrote that blind men 'feel things with perfect exactness that one might almost say that they see with their hands.'

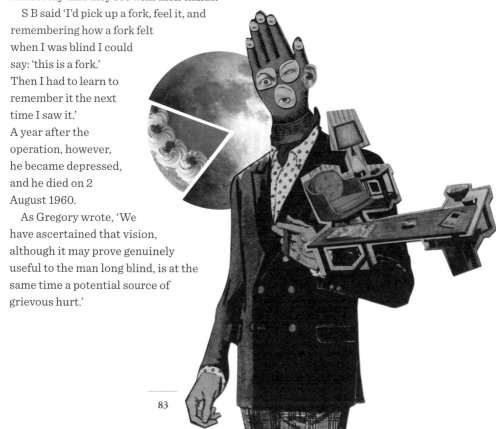

S B said 'I'd pick up a fork, feel it, and remembering how a fork felt when I was blind I could say: 'this is a fork.' Then I had to learn to remember it the next time I saw it.' A year after the operation, however, he became depressed, and he died on 2 August 1960.

As Gregory wrote, 'We have ascertained that vision, although it may prove genuinely useful to the man long blind, is at the same time a potential source of grievous hurt.'

1965

THE STUDY

RESEARCHERS:
E H Hess

SUBJECT AREA:
Experimental
psychology

CONCLUSION:
Study of the eyes
can give an indication
of what the brain
is doing.

ARE YOUR EYES THE WINDOWS TO YOUR SOUL?

PUPIL SIZE AS AN INDICATOR OF INTEREST OR EMOTION

Eckhard Hess wrote, 'When we say that someone's eyes are soft, hard, cold or warm, we are in most instances referring only to a certain aspect of that person's eyes: the size of the pupils.' The pupils are the small black holes in the centre of the eyes. Their size is controlled by the autonomic nervous system, and normally varies according to the intensity of the light; so they dilate – get bigger – in a dark room, and shrink to pinpoints in sunlight. Hess hoped that simply by measuring the dilation of the pupils while he gave volunteers things to look at or think about, he might be able to find out something about what was going on in the brain at the time. He devised a clever technique to record pupil size.

Dilated pupils

Hess had shown that most people's pupils dilate when they see something interesting or exciting. The pupils of heterosexual men and women dilate when they see a scantily clad and attractive member of the opposite sex. Homosexuals' pupils dilate when they see an attractive member of the same sex. Women's pupils dilate when they see pictures of babies, or mothers and babies.

In a more subtle study, he showed to a group of 20 men two pictures of the same woman, except that in one version her pupils were enlarged and in the other they were constricted. The men showed marked preference for the picture with enlarged pupils, even though afterwards most said the pictures were identical – but one or two said she was soft, prettier or more feminine, whereas the 'other' woman was hard, selfish or cold. They could not explain their judgements. Hess concluded that pupil size is important in non-verbal communication.

There is a drug called belladonna, which means 'beautiful lady'. Women used to put drops of it into their eyes, because they thought it made them more beautiful. The active ingredient in belladonna is atropine, which makes pupils dilate. An eyewash containing atropine used to be popular with American women until it was banned by the FDA.

The curious thing is that people don't explicitly know that bigger pupils make people look better and happier, and yet Hess showed that when asked to draw in the pupils on line drawings of sad and happy faces, both adults and children drew bigger pupils on the happy faces.

Mathematical problems

Hess went on to investigate the size of pupils while the subjects were struggling with problems in mathematics. As they thought about each problem, their pupils gradually dilated, until the point when they got the answer, and then the pupils suddenly constricted back to their normal size.

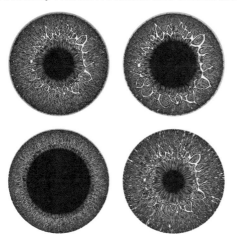

LEFT: Pupils dilating and constricting.

He asked volunteers to solve multiplications of increasing difficulty: 7 x 8   9 x 17   11 x 21   16 x 23

While they were tackling the simplest sum, their pupil sizes increased by an average of 4 per cent. When they tackled the hardest the increase was a massive 30 per cent. In all cases they then dropped back to where they had been before. In other words the amount of dilation seemed to be a measure of the amount of cognitive effort involved.

Later studies showed that pupil dilation during such tasks was greater for average students than for bright students, suggesting that the less brainy ones had to put relatively more effort into solving the problems. Hess also showed photographs of food to hungry people and to people who had just eaten. The hungry group showed greater pupil dilation; in the full group some pupils actually contracted; they really did not want more food. Kahneman and Beatty asked subjects to repeat strings of digits – for example, 538293. They found that the pupil size increased step by step as subjects heard each successive digit, and then decreased step by step as the subjects repeated each one, until they were the same size as before. The same thing happened when they were asked to call out telephone numbers from memory, although pupil dilation was greater in this memory task.

So even if the eyes are not the windows to the soul, they do tell us something interesting about what the brain is doing.

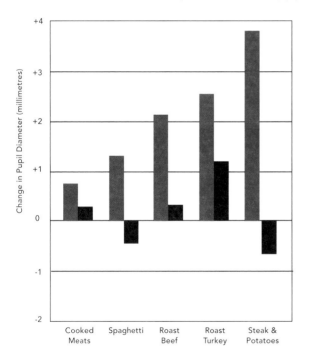

'ARE YOU SURE, DOCTOR?'

THE HOFLING HOSPITAL STUDY

1966

THE STUDY

RESEARCHERS:
C K Hofling,
E Brotzman,
S Dalrymple, N
Graves,
and C M Pierce

SUBJECT AREA:
Social psychology

CONCLUSION:
Subjects will
knowingly break
rules designed to
save lives, if ordered
to do so by an
authority figure.

The Milgram experiment (see page 78) of 1963 raised many questions about obedience and the power of authority. A few years later the American psychiatrist Charles K Hofling conducted a similar test to explore this area further. He and his colleagues were aware that doctors sometimes tread on the toes of nurses, for example by walking into an isolation unit without taking the necessary precautions, or by telling a nurse to do something that contravenes professional standards. The researchers wondered whether this behaviour would extend to nurses. Would they knowingly endanger a patient if instructed to do so by a doctor?

They carried out their experiments in 12 departments at a public psychiatric hospital and in ten departments at a private psychiatric hospital. They also asked a control group of nurses and a group of nursing students what they would do in these circumstances.

Astroten

'Dr Smith from the Psychiatric Department' (actually a stooge) telephoned each one of the 22 night nurses, and asked them whether they had any Astroten in store. Astroten was actually a

fake medicine – tablets of harmless glucose that could not cause any damage. Packets of Astroten tablets had been put in the pharmacy. 'Dr Smith' then ordered them to give 'Mr Jones' a dose of 20 milligrams of Astroten – he said it was urgent. He said he was running late, and would sign the paperwork when he got to the hospital in ten minutes' time.

The label on the bottle said *Astroten 5mg. Maximum dose 10mg. Do not exceed stated dose.* Here was the problem for the nurses: clearly 20mg was much too high a dose; the order was given over the telephone, which was against hospital policy; the medicine was unauthorized; it had not been put on the ward stock list and cleared for use; finally, 'Dr Smith' was unknown to any of the nurses.

Furthermore it was the middle of the night; the nurses were alone on night duty and therefore unable to make contact with anyone else at the hospital.

What would you do?

Suppose you had been one of those nurses. The patient's life might have been at risk. What would you do?

In the control group, 10 of the 12 nurses said they would not have given the medication, and all 21 nursing students said they would have refused. In the real live study, however, 21 out of 22 nurses would have given the medication as ordered, although in practice they were stopped at the bedside by a researcher and doctor, and explained what was going on.

Most of the telephone conversations were short, and most of the nurses did not offer much resistance; none were hostile. Afterwards 16 of them felt they should have been more resistant.

In retrospect

Only 11 of those who would have given the medicine admitted that they knew the dosage limit; the other 10 did not notice, but reckoned it must have been safe if the doctor said so. Nearly all of them admitted that they should not have contravened hospital policy: they should not have taken orders over the phone; they should have checked that 'Dr Smith' was a real doctor; and they should not have given drugs that were not authorized.

Most of them said, however, that it was normal practice to obey a doctor's instructions without question; 15 remembered similar incidents, and said that doctors got angry with nurses who resisted their orders.

Hofling and his colleagues concluded that 'Nurses will knowingly break hospital rules in a way that endangers a patient's life, if given orders by a doctor.'

Rank and Jacobson carried out a similar trial a few years later. Nurses were asked to give a non-lethal overdose of Valium to appropriate patients. In this case the nurses were able to speak to colleagues, and 16 out of 18 refused to administer the drug. This was mainly because the nurses knew of the drug's effects and had contact with colleagues, but it was also the result of an increased willingness to challenge doctors' orders, rising self-esteem among nurses and fear of lawsuits.

In 1995 Smith and MacKie reported that there was a daily 12 per cent error rate in US hospitals, and that 'Many researchers attribute such problems largely to the unquestioning deference to authority that doctors demand and nurses accept.'

1966
THE STUDY

RESEARCHERS:
N J Felipe and R
Sommer

SUBJECT AREA:
Social psychology

CONCLUSION:
Uninvited invasions
of our personal
space have a
disruptive effect.

ARE YOU A SPACE INVADER?

RESEARCH INTO PERSONAL SPACE

Personal space is that area around you which you don't like anyone else to enter uninvited. In the 1960s, the American psychologists Felipe and Sommer spent two years sitting very close to complete strangers, to see how long it would be before their subjects moved away.

They were a little worried about where to try their experiments, but eventually settled on Mendocino State Hospital, a facility for those suffering from mental illness: 'we had visions of a spatial invasion on a Central Park bench resulting in bodily assault or arrest ... [but] it seems that almost anything can be done in a mental hospital, provided it is called research.'

Getting up close and personal

The hospital was set in park like surroundings and there was easy access to the grounds; so patients could easily isolate themselves by finding a deserted area.

Felipe and Sommer carried out their research both inside and outside, choosing subjects who were male, sitting alone and not doing anything too engrossing, such as reading or playing cards. A male researcher would sit beside the subject, without saying a word, at a distance of about 15 centimetres (6 inches). If the subject moved his chair or moved further down the bench, the researcher would also move the same amount and maintain the small space between them.

The researcher either just sat there or took notes about what was going on. He also took note of other patients sitting some distance away, as controls. In all they invaded the

Intimate Zone
15–45 cm
(6–18 in)

Friend Zone
45 cm–1.2 m
(18 in–4 ft)

Social Zone
1.2–3.5 m
(4–11 ft)

space of 64 patients, for a maximum of 20 minutes each. Usually the patient would immediately turn away from the researcher, pull in his shoulders and place his elbows at his sides. Within two minutes, 36 per cent of the patients had moved away, while none of the controls had moved. At the end of 20 minutes, 64 per cent of the patients had moved. It was also found that writing notes was slightly more effective than not writing in driving victims away.

In one ward five patients were extremely territorial, and sat in the same chairs day after day. Two of these patients absolutely would not move. The researcher described them as fixed like 'the rock of Gibraltar'.

> **Personal space**

Influence of gender

Next, the researchers decided to carry out further research in a large room at a university library – where the students tended to sit as far away from one another as possible.

The researcher, female this time, would go in and deliberately sit down next to one of the female students, completely ignoring her. She then unobtrusively moved closer, so that their chairs were only about 7.5 centimetres (3 inches) apart. Then she leaned over her book, in which she took notes, and tried to maintain a distance of about 30 centimetres (12 inches) between their shoulders. This was sometimes difficult, because the library chairs were wide, and the student would occasionally slide across to the other side of her chair. If the student moved her chair away, the researcher followed by pushing her chair backwards at an angle, and then forwards again, under the pretence of adjusting her skirt.

Many of the students quickly drew in their arms, turned away, put their elbows on the table or made piles of books, handbags, and coats as barriers to separate themselves from the researcher. She sat there for a maximum of 30 minutes, at the end of which time 70 per cent of the victims had moved away. Only two of the students spoke to the researcher, and only one of the students asked the researcher to move over.

The researcher also tried sitting next to the student, but keeping a normal distance of around 38 centimetres (15 inches) between the chairs, or 60 centimetres (2 feet) between their shoulders. She also tried sitting one or two spaces away from the student, or on the opposite side of the table. None of these invasions of space had much effect.

Conclusions

Felipe and Sommer concluded that invasions of personal space have a disruptive effect, ranging from discomfort to flight, and also quoted the Australian behavioural scientist, Glen McBride, who had observed that when the dominant bird in a flock approaches, the other birds will look away and move aside to make extra space for it.

The intensity of the subject's reaction was influenced by many factors including territoriality, the dominance-submission relationship between invader and subject and the 'attribution of sexual motives to the intruder' (even though intruder and subject were always of the same gender).

However, they also noted that notions of personal space are culture-dependent: Japanese people and people from Latin countries stand closer together than Britons and Americans, for example.

1967
THE STUDY

RESEARCHERS:
S Gazzaniga and
Roger W Sperry

SUBJECT AREA:
Neuropsychology

CONCLUSION:
Splitting the brain
seems to create
two separate spheres
of consciousness.

WHAT HAPPENS WHEN A BRAIN IS CUT IN HALF?

CONSCIOUSNESS AND FUNCTIONAL HEMISPHERECTOMY

During the 1960s, some patients with severe epilepsy were treated with a drastic operation, a hemispherectomy, during which surgeons would cut through the corpus callosum (the neural fibres that connect the left and right hemispheres of the brain) to prevent seizures from affecting both sides.

After the operation, patients did not respond to touching the left side of their bodies. When an object was placed in the left hand they said it wasn't there. Astonishingly, however, they generally recovered well, and were able to lead normal lives. Their IQ, speech and problem-solving abilities were not much changed.

However, the American psychologists Michael Gazzaniga and Roger Sperry came up with some experiments to demonstrate the depth of changes that had really taken place.

When a patient held something (say a spoon) in his right hand, he could say what it was and describe it. When he held it in his left hand, he could not describe it, but given a collection of similar objects (knives, forks, etc.) he was able to match it with another spoon.

Patients were seated in front of a screen and told to fixate

RIGHT: Surgeons cut through the corpus callosum (the blue area) to separate the two sides of the brain.

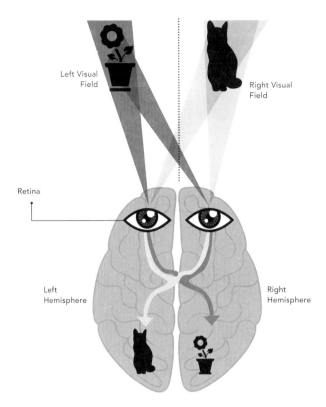

All the visual information from the left side of your visual field (from both eyes; not just the left) goes to the right hemisphere, and all the information from the right visual field goes to the left hemisphere.

on a spot in the centre. This fixation was important, for as long as they did not shift their gaze, anything flashed on the left side of the screen would go to the right hemisphere, and anything of the right side of the screen would go to the left hemisphere.

When the patient fixed his gaze on the centre of a screen and spots of light were flashed briefly across it, he said lights had been flashed only on the right side of the screen. This suggested that the right hemisphere was blind, but oddly, if the patient was told to point at the lights on the left, he could do so. Could the man see the lights, or not?

It seemed that both hemispheres could receive the visual information, but only the left hemisphere could report it with speech.

Sending information to only one side of the brain

The researchers flashed either a picture or written information to only one hemisphere, or placed an object out of sight in one of the patient's hands, so that the information went mainly to the opposite hemisphere. When the picture or word or touch of the object went to the left hemisphere, the patient could describe it normally. When information went to the right hemisphere, however, from something seen in the left visual field or held in the left hand, there was no spoken or written response – or occasionally a wild guess.

When shown a picture of an object (such as a spoon) on the left side, however, they were able to pick out a spoon with the left hand from a hidden group of objects – or a fork, if there was no spoon in the group – but they still could not say what it was.

The word HEART was flashed across the centre of the screen. Asked what they had seen, the patients said 'ART,' but asked to point with the left hand at cards marked HE and ART, they pointed at HE.

Cross-cueing

Sometimes the researchers spotted 'cross-cueing' from one hemisphere to the other. When they flashed either a red or green light to the right hemisphere, the patient would simply guess, because the right hemisphere does not control speech. When he got it wrong, however, he would frown, shake his head and say he had got it wrong, and meant the other colour. Apparently the right hemisphere saw one colour, but heard the other, and therefore precipitated a frown and a shake of the head, so the left hemisphere knew it had guessed wrongly. The right hemisphere is not always inferior. Asked to draw a cube, the patients could do it with their left hands, but not with the right; so in this case the right hemisphere was better at control.

Conclusion

Gazzaniga and Sperry came to the conclusion that separation of the hemispheres creates two independent spheres of consciousness within a single brain, but even today no one is quite sure whether that is true, nor what it means.

1968
THE STUDY

RESEARCHERS:
John Darley and
Bibb Latané

SUBJECT AREA:
Social psychology

CONCLUSION:
People in groups
are less responsive
to those in need
than individuals.

WHY DO BYSTANDERS STAND BY?

INDIVIDUAL APATHY IN EMERGENCY SITUATIONS

In March, 1964, a young woman called Kitty Genovese was stabbed to death in a New York City street. The attack went on for more than half an hour. At least 38 people saw what was happening, but not one of them intervened. No one even called the police. Why did no one help?

Perhaps it was apathy or indifference; possibly not wanting two get involved, or even fear of the attacker.

American social psychologists John Darley and Bibb Latané were fascinated by the witnesses' responses in the face of such an event, and set out to investigate the factors that had stopped people intervening.

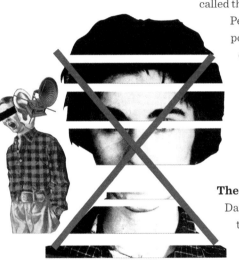

The seizure experiment

Darley and Latané asked university students to participate in a discussion about personal problems. Each would be part of a discussion group of varying size, and each of the participants was placed in a separate room communicating through microphones and headphones. The subject was unaware that all the other voices they heard were pre-recorded. Some subjects believed they were having one-to-one conversations and some believed they were in groups with up to five others. The subjects were told that the experimenter would wait in the corridor outside the room while the conversation happened.

The first pre-recorded voice would confess to the group that he was having difficulty adjusting to life in the city, and that he was also prone to serious seizures. Depending on the size of the 'group,' other voices were then heard and the subject also spoke. Then the first person spoke again reporting that he was having a seizure, and becoming louder and more incoherent. There was a choking sound, and then deathly quiet.

Almost all the subjects were convinced the fit was real. Of those that thought they were the only person to have heard the attack, 100 per cent reported the fit, with 85 per cent running to the corridor before the 'victim' had stopped speaking. Of the subjects that thought they were in a group of six, only 62 per cent of them reported the fit at all. However, these students did not appear to be apathetic or indifferent – as was previously assumed of unresponsive bystanders – they were visibly shaken with trembling hands and sweating palms.

Not so safe in numbers

The research team demonstrated that not only were people in groups less likely to respond to an emergency than individuals, but the response was inversely proportional to the number of witnesses. The greater the number of bystanders, the less likely it was that anyone would help.

Darley and Latané concluded that when only one person witnesses an emergency, any help must come from that person and the pressure is on to do something. When there are more witnesses that pressure is dispersed and individuals assume that someone else will take action; or they may worry that their intervention will hinder the efforts of those more qualified.

The scientific context of the situation is also significant, since, as in the Milgram experiment (see page 78), subjects also reported concerns about disrupting or halting the test.

1968
THE STUDY

RESEARCHERS:
Robert Rosenthal and
Lenore Jacobson

SUBJECT AREA:
Social psychology

CONCLUSION:
High expectations can
lead to better results.

CAN RESULTS IMPROVE BY SIMPLY EXPECTING THEM TO?

THE PYGMALION EFFECT AND THE POWER OF SELF-FULFILLING PROPHECIES

There are many anecdotes about self-fulfilling prophecies; but could there be any scientific evidence to support the superstition?

In 1963 Lenore Jacobson was the principal of an elementary school in San Francisco; she approached Harvard psychologist Robert Rosenthal after reading an article of his. Together they wondered whether something as important as a child's success at school could be affected by a teacher's expectations.

In the schoolroom

They went into a public elementary school, which they called Oak School, where the teachers divided each grade into three tracks: fast, medium and slow; in general there were more boys and more Mexican children in the slow track. The teachers assigned the tracks on the basis of each child's reading ability and performance in tests.

The researchers tested 350 children using what they grandiloquently described as the 'Harvard Test of Inflected Acquisition' and told the teachers that this was an assessment designed to predict 'spurting' or 'blooming' in children.

The test was actually Flanagan's Test Of General Ability (TOGA), and tested IQ in terms of verbal ability and reasoning. For example, at one level children were shown pictures of a suit jacket, a flower, an envelope, an apple and a glass of water, and were asked to mark with a crayon 'the thing you can eat'.

Picking the 'spurters'

The researchers did not tell the teachers the results, and instead chose one fifth of the students, from slow, medium and fast tracks, at random and told each teacher which of the children in their classes were predicted by the 'Harvard Test' to put on a spurt in the following year, and to do better than the others in the class. They also made sure to ask the teachers not to mention the test to either the children or their parents.

Results

A year later they gave all the children the same IQ test. All six grades showed an improvement in IQ; the average gain was more than eight points, but the spurters did much better than their peers. They gained on average 12.2 points, 3.8 more than the rest. The effect was almost entirely confined to grades 1 and 2, where 21 per cent of spurters gained more than 30 IQ points, compared with 5 per cent of non-spurters.

Grade	Control		'Spurters'		
	Number	Increase	Number	Increase	Advantage
1	48	+12.0	7	+27.4	+15.4
2	47	+7.0	12	+16.5	+9.5
3	40	+5.0	14	+5.0	0
4	49	+2.2	12	+5.6	+3.4
5	26	+17.5	9	+17.4	-0.1
6	45	+10.7	11	+10.0	-0.7
Total	255	+8.4	65	+12.2	+3.8

The fact that the effect was confined to the first two grades may possibly have been because teachers have most influence over the youngest children. They are more malleable and more capable of change, or they may not yet have an established reputation in the school.

There was no significant difference between children in different tracks; that is those in the slow and medium tracks did just as well as those in the fast track. Girls did slightly better than boys in the reasoning test: among the spurters, the girls showed a large advantage of 17.9 points over the non-spurters, while the boys actually did worse than the average.

Conclusions

Rosenthal and Jacobson observed what has come to be described as the 'Pygmalion effect.' When teachers expected certain children to show greater development, those children did just that: a 'self-fulfilling prophecy was in evidence.'

But why was there any effect at all? It's possible that the teachers had a different attitude towards the spurters or gave them more attention, subconsciously behaving in ways that would encourage the students to achieve.

Curiously, this study was allegedly inspired by a performing horse. At the start of the twentieth century the horse, known as Clever Hans, became famous for his apparent ability to read, spell and carry out simple mental arithmetic. When challenged to calculate 3+4, for example, Clever Hans would tap his hoof seven times.

The psychologist Oskar Pfungst investigated the case and concluded that the animal was probably being guided by the subconscious responses of his audience. When he reached the right answer their reactions would change, and Hans would know he had done enough tapping.

WHAT DO BABIES DO IN 'STRANGE SITUATIONS'?

SEPARATION ANXIETY IN BABIES

THE STUDY

RESEARCHERS:
Mary D Salter
Ainsworth and Silvia
M Bell

SUBJECT AREA:
Developmental
psychology

CONCLUSION:
Infants need their
mothers as a secure
base from which to
explore the world.

Harry Harlow's controversial experiments (see page 64) into maternal attachment had shown that baby monkeys would explore their surroundings in the presence of a soft, mother-like figure, but in the absence of such a figure they became miserable and withdrawn.

Mary Ainsworth and Silvia Bell wanted to find out whether human babies behave in similar ways; so they set up a 'strange situation' in their laboratory. Their room had a large space in the middle, and three chairs – one heaped with toys at the far end of the room and two others, near the door, for mother and a female stranger. The baby was put down in the middle of the triangle formed by the chairs. Then they proceeded with eight episodes, identical for each baby:

Episode 1 (M, B, O). Mother (M), with an observer (O), carried the baby (B) into the room, and then O left.

Episode 2 (M, B; three minutes). M put B down, then sat quietly in her chair, participating only if B sought her attention.

Episode 3 (S, M, B). A stranger (S) entered, sat quietly for one minute, conversed with M for one minute, and then gradually approached B, showing him a toy. After three minutes M left the room unobtrusively.

Episode 4 (S, B; three minutes). If B was happily engaged in play, S was non-participant. If B was inactive, she tried to interest him in the toys. If B was distressed, she tried to distract or comfort him. If he could not be comforted, the episode was then curtailed.

Episode 5 (M, B). M entered, paused in the doorway to give B an opportunity for a spontaneous response. S then left unobtrusively. Once B was again settled in play with the toys M left again, after pausing to say 'bye-bye.'

Episode 6 (B alone; three minutes). The baby was left alone, unless he was so distressed that the episode had to be curtailed.

Episode 7 (S, B; three minutes). S entered and behaved as in episode 4, unless distress prompted curtailment.

Episode 8 (M, B). M returned, S left, and after the reunion had been observed, the situation was terminated.

They carried out these experiments with 56 babies, each 11 months old, all 'family-reared infants of white, middle-class parents'. Observers watched through a one-way mirror, and took notes.

Exploratory behaviour

The researchers were particularly interested in how much the baby crawled about ('locomotion'), played with the toys ('manipulation') and looked at the toys and around the room. When the stranger came in for episode 3 there was a sharp drop in all forms of exploratory behaviour. Looking and playing increased again when the mother came back in, but the stranger failed to increase them in episodes 4 and 7; indeed the exploratory behaviour dropped to its lowest level in 7, although it is possible they were tired by then, and bored of the room.

During episode 2 the baby spent a lot of time looking at the toys, glancing only occasionally at its mother, to make sure she was still there. In episode 3, however, the baby spent more time looking at the stranger.

Crying, clinging and resisting contact

There was little crying in episode 2, suggesting that the strange situation itself was not very alarming. There was some crying in episode 4, when the mother left, less in episode 5 and much more in episode 6, which the stranger was unable to reduce in 7, suggesting that it was the mother's absence that was most distressing, rather than just being alone.

In episodes 2 and 3 the baby made only slight efforts to cling to its mother, but was much more enthusiastic after separation and reunion in episodes 5 and especially 8.

Some babies resisted contact, especially with the stranger. This may have been caused by fear of her, but Ainsworth and Bell think it more likely it was because the baby was angry at the mother's departure.

Conclusions

Babies are generally attached to their mothers. When mother is in the room, the baby will approach new things and explore them, which is what happened in this study; the babies were not terrified by the strange situation; they did not cling to their mothers. When the mother leaves, the baby explores less and shows more signs of attachment behaviour, including crying and searching.

As the researchers wrote, 'Provided that there is no threat of separation, the infant is likely to be able to use his mother as a secure base from which to explore, manifesting no alarm in even a strange situation, as long as she is present.'

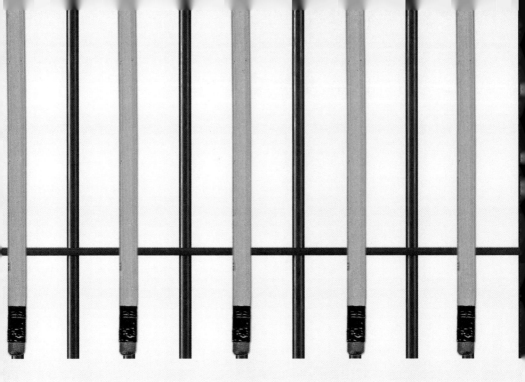

CHAPTER 5: The cognitive revolution: 1971-1980

In his 1967 book, *Cognitive Psychology*, the German scientist Ulric Gustav Neisser questioned the paradigms of behaviourism and started other psychologists thinking.

They began to realize that to find out what makes people tick they needed to investigate what goes on in the mind. Before long the label 'cognitive psychology' began to embrace perception, language, attention and memory, as well as thinking. This was not entirely new,

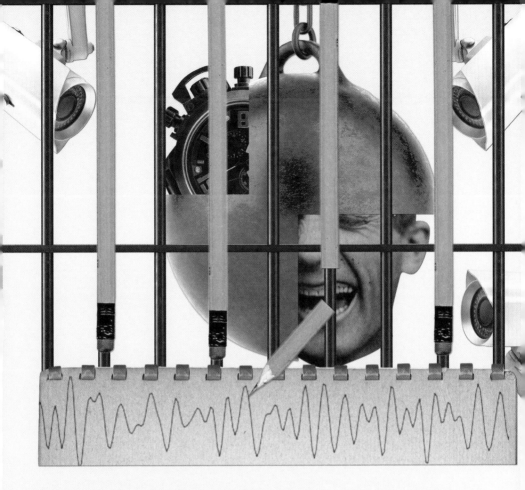

but the time now seemed ripe for cognition to creep into every area of psychology, and to change the way research was done.

Peter Wason's card tricks teased out the way we think about what is true; Elizabeth Loftus's work on false memory provoked decades of further research; while Daniel Kahneman and Amos Tversky showed us why we make bad decisions.

1971

THE STUDY

RESEARCHER:

Philip Zimbardo

SUBJECT AREA:

Social psychology

CONCLUSION:

The harsh prison
situation, rather
than their individual
personalities, caused
participants to
behave in cruel
or violent ways.

CAN GOOD PEOPLE
TURN BAD?

SITUATIONAL INFLUENCES ON BEHAVIOUR
AND THE STANFORD PRISON EXPERIMENT

Philip Zimbardo was a student at James Monroe High School at the same time as his fellow New Yorker Stanley Milgram (see page 78). After completing his PhD he taught at Yale, NYU and Columbia, before joining the faculty at Stanford, where he was to carry out the experiment for which he is now best known.

Zimbardo was interested in claims of brutality and violence reported in prisons and wanted to explore the question of whether prisoners are inherently violent and those who become prison guards are naturally authoritarian, and perhaps sadistic; or whether these traits evolve and come to the fore simply because of the prison environment.

Building a makeshift prison

He advertised in local newspapers for male volunteers for a psychological study of prison life. He interviewed 70 applicants, and chose 24 college students: healthy, middle-class boys. They were told that the study would last for one or two weeks, and that they would be paid $15 a day. Half were randomly chosen to be prisoners and the other half guards.

Meanwhile, the experimenters held consultations with experts, including a man who had spent 17 years in prison, and constructed a 'prison' in the basement of Stanford University's Psychology Department. Three rooms, each just big enough for three beds, were fitted with heavyweight doors made from steel bars and given cell numbers. The corridor became the 'exercise yard', and a small wardrobe became 'The Hole' – a solitary confinement cell.

If they wanted to go to the toilet, the prisoners would have to ask permission, and then be blindfolded and led down the hallway. The rooms were bugged for sound and there was a small hole through which proceedings could be videotaped.

Each 'prisoner' was picked up at home, charged, warned of his legal rights, spread-eagled against the police car, searched and handcuffed, while startled neighbours watched, goggle-eyed. At the 'jail,' he was searched, stripped naked and then deloused with a spray – a procedure designed to humiliate. He was then given a uniform: a stocking cap and a smock to wear at all times, without underwear, and with his prison ID number stencilled on the front and back. A heavy chain was bolted around his right ankle.

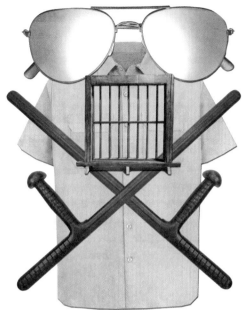

ABOVE: The guards were issued with khaki uniforms and dark mirror glasses.

Humiliation

Real male prisoners don't wear dresses, but they do feel humiliated. Zimbardo aimed to produce similar effects quickly. The stocking cap was a substitute for having all the hair shaved off, which is what happens in real prisons. The chain was used to remind them of the oppressiveness of the environment, and tended to keep them awake at night.

The guards were issued with khaki uniforms, dark mirror glasses, whistles and police batons, but were given no specific instructions or training.

The experiment began with nine prisoners. Additionally,

there were nine guards who worked in eight-hour shifts, three on each shift. At 2:30 a.m. on the first night the prisoners were woken by blasting whistles for the first of many 'counts.' Some of the prisoners were not yet fully into their roles, and would not accept discipline from the guards, who retaliated by making them do push-ups, which were made more difficult by standing on the prisoners' backs.

Prisoner rebellion

The first day went quietly, but on the morning of the second day the prisoners rebelled. They ripped off their stocking caps, and barricaded themselves inside their cells by jamming their beds against the doors. The guards subdued the rebels with icy jets of carbon dioxide from fire extinguishers; they stripped the prisoners naked, took their beds away and put the ringleaders into solitary confinement.

The guards then decided on psychological warfare to regain control. They took three prisoners who had been least rebellious, put them in rooms with beds and gave them special food, while the others watched. This set the other prisoners against the favoured three, and caused most of their frustration and anger to be targeted at one another, instead of at the guards.

Meanwhile, the guards became more heavy-handed, and denied even the smallest of privileges; sometimes they refused prisoners permission to go to the toilet, and left them a bucket to use in their cells. The stench became overpowering. Within 36 hours one of the prisoners showed acute emotional disturbance. Even though the experimenters had begun behaving like prison warders, and initially did not believe the prisoner was in real distress, they eventually allowed him to leave the experiment.

As the days passed, the guards became gradually more brutal and sadistic, especially at night, when they thought no one was watching. Meanwhile, the prisoners, who had at first fought with the guards, gradually broke down emotionally. One developed a rash all over his body. By the end of the study they were, as Zimbardo put it, 'disintegrated, both as a group and as individuals. There was no longer any group unity; just a bunch of isolated individuals hanging on.'

Termination

The situation became so bad that Zimbardo had to stop the experiment on the sixth day. All the prisoners were happy about this, but not the guards.

Zimbardo wrote:

> *After observing our simulated prison for only six days, we could understand how prisons dehumanize people, turning them into objects and instilling in them feelings of hopelessness. And as for guards, we realized how ordinary people could be readily transformed from the good Dr Jekyll to the evil Mr Hyde.*
>
> *The question now is how to change our institutions so that they promote human values rather than destroy them.*

1971

THE STUDY

RESEARCHERS:

Peter Wason and
Diana Shapiro

SUBJECT AREA:

Cognition, decision-
making

CONCLUSION:

We struggle with
abstract problems,
but the same
problem becomes
easy when expressed
in concrete terms.

CAN YOU PICK THE LOGICAL ANSWER?

**WASON'S SELECTION TASK: ABSTRACT
REASONING IN CONCRETE TERMS**

Try this logic problem:

Every card is coloured on one side and has a number on the other. All blue cards should have an even number on the back. Which of these cards would you have to turn over to find out whether that is true?

Beware; at least 70 per cent of people get this wrong. Which cards would you turn over?

Peter Wason was interested in how people tackle logical problems, and first introduced some like this in 1966. He explained how to approach it in terms of pure logic, which you may or may not find helpful.

In this example, p is the blueness of the card, and q is the evenness of the number; so p is true for the first card and false for the second, and q is true for the fourth card, but false for the third. Therefore you have to turn over the blue card, to see whether it has an even number on the back. You also have to turn over the 3 card, because that is an example of q being false; 3 is not an even number. Turning over the 8 card does not help, for if it is blue that is fine, but if it is pink (or any other colour) that is still fine; it does not contravene the rule.

So the correct cards to turn over are blue and 3.

Wason and Shapiro gave students a total of 24 tests like this one. There were only seven correct answers (29 per cent). The students were too concerned with verifying the rule, and ignored the possibility of falsification. In other words, they ignored the chance to falsify the rule by turning over the q false card.

The researchers wondered whether the problem might be easier if it was related to the real world, and devised what they called 'thematic' problems. They divided 32 undergraduate students into two groups. Those in the abstract group were given a task like the one above: four cards had a letter on one side and a number of the other. They were showing D, K, 3 and 7. The rule was 'Every card with a D on one side has a 3 on the other.' Which cards do you have to turn over to decide whether it was true or false?

Can you solve it? The answer is at the end of this entry.

Those in the thematic group were told that the experimenter had made four journeys on particular days. She claimed that every time she went to Manchester she travelled by car. Four cards represented her journeys; each had a town on one side and a mode of transport on the other: which cards would they have to turn over to verify her claim?

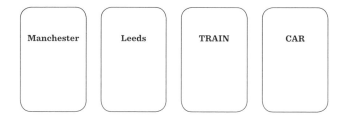

Results

The abstract group averaged only two correct (12.5 per cent). The thematic group did much better, with ten correct (62.5 per cent). The researchers concluded that the thematic problem is easier because it deals with concrete material rather than abstract letters and numbers, and also has a relationship between the words; they are all about travel, and situations that could happen in real life.

But the easiest of all is a situation that happens all the time when you go out drinking. Suppose you are in a bar, where no one under the age of 21 is allowed to drink beer. Each card represents one drinker:

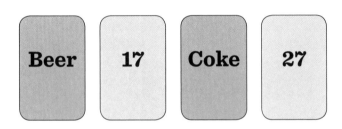

Which cards do you have to turn over to find out whether these four are obeying the law? You should find this one easy.

The conclusion seems to be that we can solve such problems easily when they involve social compliance. This might be because we are more familiar with social situations, or because our brains have evolved to solve social problems, rather than abstract ones.

The correct answers are D and 7,
Manchester and train, and Beer and 17.

CAN PSYCHIATRISTS TELL IF YOU'RE SANE?

THE ROSENHAN EXPERIMENT AND 'BEING SANE IN INSANE PLACES'

1973
THE STUDY
RESEARCHER:
David L. Rosenhan
SUBJECT AREA:
Social psychology
CONCLUSION:
Professionals in some psychiatric hospitals cannot distinguish the sane from the insane and exhibit dangerous levels of dehumanization.

In 1973, American psychologist David L Rosenhan published 'On Being Sane in Insane Places' which detailed his study into the validity of psychiatric diagnoses. Rosenhan persuaded eight perfectly sane people to admit themselves to different psychiatric hospitals across the United States. These 'pseudopatients' comprised a psychology student, three academic psychologists, a paediatrician, a psychiatrist, a painter and a housewife; three female, five male. They all used false names, and those working in mental health gave different occupations.

Hearing voices

First the pseudopatients called the hospital for an appointment. The only symptom they described was that they heard voices. They said the voices were often unclear, but seemed to say 'empty', 'hollow' and 'thud'. Otherwise they told the truth about their lives, families and relationships.

They were all admitted immediately, which was worrying, but thereafter they gave no further signs of any abnormality. When asked by staff how they were feeling, they said they were fine, and no longer heard voices. They were all keen to be discharged, and were described in nurses' reports as 'friendly', 'cooperative' and 'exhibited no abnormal indications'. They accepted medication, although they did not swallow it. In total they were given 2,100 pills of a variety of drugs, but flushed them down the toilet, where they often found pills deposited by real patients. And yet in spite of their

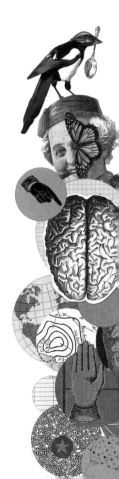

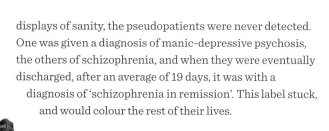

displays of sanity, the pseudopatients were never detected. One was given a diagnosis of manic-depressive psychosis, the others of schizophrenia, and when they were eventually discharged, after an average of 19 days, it was with a diagnosis of 'schizophrenia in remission'. This label stuck, and would colour the rest of their lives.

Writing notes

They spent a great deal of time writing notes about their experiences, which at first they kept secret. Soon, however, it became apparent that the staff were not interested and never looked at the notes; so often they wrote them openly, in the day room. One nurse noted every day in the pseudopatient's case notes 'Indulges in writing behaviour'. This was clearly perceived as a symptom of schizophrenia.

In each hospital, the staff were strictly segregated from the patients. Staff had their own living space, including dining facilities, bathrooms and assembly places. The pseudopatients called these glassed quarters 'the cage', and noted that the staff emerged on average just 11.3 per cent of the time.

When they did come out they were extremely unwilling to indulge in conversation. If a pseudopatient approached with a question such as 'Pardon me, Dr X, when am I likely to be discharged?' the most common response was 'Good morning, Dave. How are you today?' and walked on without waiting for an answer.

Rosenhan writes vividly about depersonalization: 'powerlessness was evident everywhere. The patient is deprived of many of his legal rights by dint of his psychiatric commitment. . . . Personal privacy is minimal. Patient quarters and possessions can be entered and examined by any staff member, for whatever reason . . . His personal hygiene and waste evacuation are often monitored. The water closets may have no doors.'

Rumbled by patients

Even though they were never spotted as frauds by the staff, they were found out by other patients. During the first three hospitalizations, one third of the patients on the admissions ward were suspicious: some, having watched the note-taking, even said things like, 'You're not crazy. You're a journalist, or a professor. You're checking up on the hospital.'

As Rosenhan writes:

The fact that the patients often recognized normality when staff did not raises important questions. Failure to detect sanity during the course of hospitalization may be due to the fact that physicians . . . are more inclined to call a healthy person sick . . . than a sick person healthy . . . it is clearly more dangerous to misdiagnose illness than health. Better to err on the side of caution, to suspect illness even among the healthy.

Whenever the ratio of what is known to what needs to be known approaches zero, we tend to invent 'knowledge' and assume that we understand more than we actually do. We seem unable to acknowledge that we simply don't know. The needs for diagnosis and remediation of behavioural and emotional problems are enormous. But . . . we continue to label patients 'schizophrenic', 'manic-depressive' and 'insane', as if in those words we had captured the essence of understanding. The facts of the matter are that we have known for a long time that diagnoses are often not useful or reliable, but we have nevertheless continued to use them.

THE STUDY

RESEARCHERS:
Mark R Lepper, David Greene and Richard E Nisbett

SUBJECT AREA:
Social psychology

CONCLUSION:
Rewards can undermine a child's natural interest in certain activities.

ARE CHILDREN PUT OFF BY BRIBES?

THE TROUBLE WITH GOLD STARS

Children in school are often given gold stars, and other extrinsic rewards, and there is a danger that these rewards may actually reduce enthusiasm: 'I am doing this arithmetic in order to get a star' – rather than because it's interesting or fun.

Lepper and his colleagues set out to test this theory in a nursery on the Stanford University campus. They chose a group of white, middle-class children who were known to be interested in drawing, and divided them randomly into three groups. Each of the children in Group A was told in advance that he or she would receive a reward in the shape of a handsome Good Player Award certificate embellished with a gold star, a red ribbon and the names of the child and the school. Each of the children in Group B were given the same type of award, but did not know about it until after they had finished drawing. Children in Group C received no award.

The experiment phase one

For each trial a single child was brought into the room and invited by an experimenter to do some drawing with a set of multicoloured fluorescent pens, which were not normally available to the children. If the child was in Group A the experimenter produced a sample award, and said the child would get one for his or her drawing. Children from other groups were simply invited to start drawing.

After six minutes the experimenter interrupted, and for children from Groups A and B presented the Good Player Award, after writing the child's name and school on it. Together they then pinned the award on a special 'Honour Roll' board 'so that everyone will know what a good player you are'.

The experiment phase two

One week later, the researchers began the second phase of the experiment. First, teachers placed on a small hexagonal table the set of special pens, and white paper. The classroom also contained a number of other activities, including building blocks, easels, housekeeping equipment and sometimes playdough. When the group of children came in they were free to do anything they liked. For the first hour, the activities at the hexagonal table were carefully monitored by observers from behind a one-way mirror.

In the end a total of 51 children – 19 boys and 32 girls – completed the experiment. Of these 18 were in Group A, 18 in Group B, and 15 in Group C.

Prediction of outcome

The researchers predicted that the promise of a reward would make the children less interested in the task. This was precisely borne out by the results. The children in Group A, who had been told in advance that they would get an award, were afterwards much less interested in drawing with the coloured pens; in fact they spent only about half as much time drawing as the others. There was no significant difference between girls and boys.

Children in both Groups B and C showed slightly more interest in drawing with coloured pens than they had before the experiment began.

The pictures drawn by the children during the experimental trials were rated for quality, on a scale of 1 to

5, by three judges who did not know which groups the artists had been in. The average scores were Group A, 2.18; Group B, 2.85; Group C, 2.69. In other words, having been told they would get an extrinsic reward, the children in Group A drew pictures that were significantly less good than the others.

Extrinsic vs intrinsic

The researchers concluded that their findings:

> ... *have important practical implications for situations in which extrinsic incentives are used to enhance or maintain children's interest in activities of some initial interest to the child. Such situations, we would suggest, occur frequently in traditional classrooms where systems of extrinsic rewards – whether grades, gold stars, or the awarding of special privileges – are applied as a matter of course to an entire class of children.*

> *Many of the activities we ask children to attempt in school, in fact, are of intrinsic interest to at least some of the children; one effect of presenting these activities within a system of extrinsic incentives, the present study suggests, is to undermine the intrinsic interest in these activities of at least those children who had some interest to begin with.*

HOW ACCURATE ARE YOUR MEMORIES?

FALSE MEMORIES AND THE MISINFORMATION EFFECT

1974

THE STUDY

RESEARCHER:
Elizabeth F Loftus

SUBJECT AREA:
Memory

CONCLUSION:
Our memories of events can be affected by information we receive after the fact.

Do you think your memories are accurate and unchanging? If so, you are probably wrong. When someone says 'I saw it with my own eyes,' people are inclined to believe it. However, between the time you witness an event and the time you recount it to someone else, your memory may change a great deal, especially if an interested person asks you leading questions.

Professor Elizabeth Loftus found that when she staged an event, and then asked individuals about it afterwards, they often all gave different accounts.

Loftus explains that 'When we experience an event, we do not simply file a memory, and then on some later occasion retrieve it and read off what we've stored. Rather, at the time of recall or recognition, we reconstruct the event, using information from many sources. These include both the original perception of the event and inferences drawn later, after the fact. Over a period of time information from these sources may integrate, so that a witness becomes unable to say how he knows a specific detail. He has only a single, unified memory.'

In other words, the brain takes in what it actually experiences of the event, and makes up a plausible story to account for what seems to have happened. Later, if other information or suggestions come in, the brain may reconstruct the memory to fit the new input. Loftus had noticed that the form of questions asked of witnesses seemed to change their memories, and she set up an experiment to find out how easily

this could happen. She showed 100 students a short film depicting a multiple car accident.

Leading questions

After seeing the film the students filled out a questionnaire which included six critical questions: three about items that had appeared in the film, and three others about items that had not.

For half the subjects the critical questions were of the form 'Did you see *a* broken headlight?' For the other half the critical questions were of the form 'Did you see *the* broken headlight?' The second of these questions implies that there was a broken headlight, whether or not one actually appeared in the film. Witnesses who received questions with 'the' were much more likely to report having seen something that had not really appeared in the film: 15 per cent in the 'the' group said 'yes' when asked about a non-existent item, while only 7 per cent of the 'a' group said 'yes.' In other words, just changing from 'a' to 'the' seemed actually to have altered the memories of 8 per cent of the students. Alternatively, 38 per cent in the 'a' group answered 'Don't know', as opposed to 13 per cent in the 'the' group.

To find out whether other small changes in the question could affect quantitative judgements she showed 45 subjects seven films of traffic accidents. For some of the viewers of one film, she asked in a questionnaire 'about how fast were the cars going when they *hit/ smashed/ collided/ bumped/ contacted* each other?' The resulting estimates varied considerably.

Memory adjustment

Another group of students were shown a similar film and asked how fast the cars were going when they 'hit' or 'smashed into' each other. One week later, they were asked whether they had seen any broken glass, although there had been none in the film. Twice as many of the students who had been asked a question with 'smashed' said they had seen broken glass as those who had been asked a question with 'hit'. In other words, their memories of the film had apparently been altered just because they had been asked a question with a slight change of words.

Average speed estimates for various verbs	
smashed	65.7 kmph/40.8 mph
collided	63.2 kmph/39.3 mph
bumped	61.3 kmph/38.1 mph
hit	54.7 kmph/34.0 mph
contacted	51.2 kmph/31.8 mph

Loftus concludes:

Eyewitnesses are inaccurate in estimating not only speed but also time and distance. Yet in courts of law they must make quantitative judgements all the time. Accident investigators, police officers, lawyers, reporters and others who must interrogate eyewitnesses would do well to keep in mind the subtle suggestibility that words carry with them. When you question an eyewitness, what he saw may not be what you get.

False memories

The phenomenon of a person's recall becoming less accurate because of post-event suggestion or information has come to be known as the 'misinformation effect', and Loftus's work led to decades of research into the condition of 'false memory'. There is considerable danger that interrogators, not only in courts of law and in police stations but also in the armed services, can plant false memories, either by accident or by design.

THE STUDY

RESEARCHERS:
Amos Tversky and
Daniel Kahneman
SUBJECT AREA:
Cognition, decision-
making
CONCLUSION:
When an outcome is
unknown, cognitive
bias can cause us to
make poor decisions.

HOW DO YOU MAKE
TRICKY DECISIONS?

'HEURISTICS' AND ASSESSING
POTENTIAL RISK

Most people find decisions difficult when they don't know the exact outcomes, and they often get them wrong. Psychologists Daniel Kahneman and Amos Tversky began collaborating by looking at contradictions in human behaviour.

Heuristics

The researchers found that when people make judgements about uncertain futures they tend to use 'heuristics', mental shortcuts that rely on simple, efficient rules, often focusing on one aspect of a problem while ignoring others.

For example, suppose you are told that 'Steve is shy and withdrawn, invariably helpful; a meek and tidy soul, he has a need for order and structure, and a passion for detail'. You are also told that Steve may be a farmer, salesman, airline pilot, librarian or doctor. Which do you think is the most likely?

You might be tempted to say librarian, but there are many more farmers than librarians, and therefore Steve is in fact more likely to be a farmer than a librarian, in spite of his personal characteristics. This is the 'representativeness heuristic'.

In an experiment, a group of students were told about one man in a group of 100 professionals: 'Dick is married with no children. A man of high ability and high motivation, he promises to be quite successful in his field. He is well-liked by his colleagues'.

Half the students were told that the group comprised 70

engineers and 30 lawyers; the other half were told it was 30 engineers and 70 lawyers. When asked whether Dick was likely to be a lawyer or an engineer, they all said it was 50-50. They ignored the fact that he was much more likely to be one of the larger group: the chances were 70-30, one way or the other.

Consider the letter K. In a typical chunk of English prose, is the letter K more likely to occur as the first letter in a word or as the third letter? What do you think?

This question was posed to 152 subjects, and 105 (69 per cent) said it was more likely to be the first letter. In fact K typically turns up twice as often in position three as in position one. The problem is that thinking of words beginning with K is easy, while thinking of words with K as the third letter is much harder. The same is true of L, N, R and V. This is called the 'availability heuristic', because it relies on the immediate examples that come to mind.

Regression towards the mean

Imagine that a large group of children has been examined with two equivalent versions of an aptitude test. Suppose you choose the ten best on the first version, then you will probably find they did worse on the second version. On the other hand if you choose the ten children who did worst on the first version, you will find they did better on the second. This is called 'regression to the mean', and was first discussed by Francis Galton in the nineteenth century.

The ten best may really be better than everyone else in the class, but they may well have done slightly better on this test just by luck; they are likely to be closer to the average, or mean. The consequence is that the ten best are likely to move back again, and the ten worst to move forward.

The researchers point out that ignoring this can lead to dangerous consequences:

In a discussion of flight training, experienced instructors noted that praise for an exceptionally smooth landing is typically followed by a poorer landing on the next try, while harsh criticism after a rough landing is usually followed by an improvement on the next try. The instructors concluded that verbal rewards are bad for learning, while verbal punishments are good, contrary to accepted psychological doctrine. This conclusion is unwarranted because of the presence of a regression towards the mean.

Probabilities of Death in US From Various Causes (per cent)		
Cause	Subject Estimates	Real probability
Heart Disease	22	34
Cancer	18	23
Other Natural Causes	33	35
All Natural Causes	73	92
Accident	32	5
Murder	10	1
Other Unnatural Causes	11	2
All Unnatural Causes	53	8

How will you die?

The researchers asked 120 Stanford graduates how likely they thought they were to die from various causes. This table lists the averages of their answers. They slightly underestimated probabilities for natural causes, and vastly overestimated probabilities for unnatural causes. It looks as if they spent too much time worrying about accidents and murder, and perhaps not enough worrying about their health.

Tversky and Kahneman conclude: 'analysis of the heuristics that a person uses . . . may tell us whether his judgement is likely to be too high or too low. We believe that such analyses could be used to reduce the prevalence of errors in human judgement under uncertainty.'

Their work has led to a huge amount of research on human bias in decision-making.

CAN SHEER TERROR BE SEXY?

HEIGHTENED SEXUAL ATTRACTION UNDER CONDITIONS OF HIGH ANXIETY

1974
THE STUDY

RESEARCHER:
Donald G Dutton
and Arthur P Aron

SUBJECT AREA:
Experimental
psychology

CONCLUSION:
There is a definite
connection between
the body's response
to fear and arousal.

If you were frightened, would you find potential partners more attractive? Can you tell the difference between sexual arousal and sheer terror?

There is some evidence to suggest that sexual arousal is associated with strong emotion, or even increased by strong emotion; that is why people take their partners to dangerous funfair rides and scary films. In fact we may simply be unable to distinguish the separate emotions.

The Capilano bridges

Researchers Donald Dutton and Arthur Aron devised a clever way to investigate the relationship between fear and sexual arousal. They found two bridges over the Capilano River in North Vancouver, Canada. One – the control bridge – was a wide, solid, cedarwood bridge with high hand rails, 3 metres (10 feet) above a small stream. The other – the experimental bridge – was the Capilano Canyon Suspension Bridge. This was a long, narrow bridge, made of wooden boards hanging on wire cables, 70 metres (230 feet) above a raging torrent. The handrails were low, and the bridge swayed and wobbled when pedestrians attempted to cross it. Many of those who crossed the suspension bridge walked slowly and carefully, hanging on to the handrail.

The subjects were men who were judged to be between 18 and 35, and happened to be walking across one of the bridges, without a female companion. As the subject walked across the bridge, he was approached by an interviewer, who asked him, as part of a psychology experiment, to fill in a short questionnaire. The first page had basic questions about age, sex, education, previous visits to the bridge, and so on. On the second page they were asked to write a short dramatic story based on a picture of a young woman covering her face with one hand and reaching out with the other.

The stories were later scored for sexual content, ranging from 1 for no sexual content, through 3 for a kiss, to 5 for any mention of intercourse.

Did the sex of the interviewer make a difference?

When the subjects had finished their questionnaires, the interviewers thanked them and offered to explain the experiment in detail when there was more time. They offered their phone numbers, and invited the men to call if they wanted to talk further.

What differences would you expect from the sex of the interviewer? The interviewers were students – some male, some female. Most of the men who were approached agreed to take part, especially with a female interviewer.

The results showed that men were more inclined to take part if the interviewer was female; also that being interviewed

Interviewer	Number taking part	No. accepting phone no.	No. who phoned	Sexiness of story
M – control bridge	22/42	6/22	1	0.61
M – scary bridge	23/51	7/23	2	0.80
F – control bridge	22/33	16/22	2	1.41
F – scary bridge	23/33	18/23	9	2.47

on the frightening suspension bridge seemed to make the female interviewer appear more attractive. The men had definitely been aroused. Not only did they write sexier stories than the others; many more of them called her afterwards.

In other words there is a definite connection between fear and arousal, or to put it another way, you cannot tell whether the adrenaline coursing through you is caused by sexual arousal or sheer terror.

THE STUDY

RESEARCHERS:
William R. Miller
and Martin Seligman

SUBJECT AREA:
Behavioural
psychology

CONCLUSION:
A perceived absence
of control over
negative events
may lead to clinical
depression.

CAN DOGS GET DEPRESSED?

LEARNED HELPLESSNESS AND DEPRESSION

As a research student working with the experimental psychologist Richard L Solomon, Martin Seligman began working with dogs in an extension of the work of Pavlov (page 19). He placed a dog in a box that was divided in half by a low barrier, chest-high to the dog. After a while, the dog would get a brief electric shock, and then another and

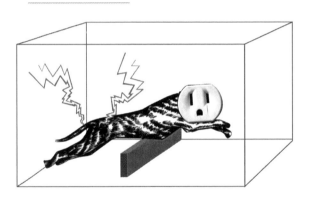

another. If the dog jumped over the barrier into the other half of the box, the shocks stopped. Then the shocks started there instead, and to stop them the dog had to jump back to the first side. Soon the dogs learned to jump the barrier as soon as they felt the first shock. This was known as operant conditioning. Seligman then exposed another group of dogs to unavoidable intermittent electric shocks. When he put one of these dogs into the divided box, they never did learn to jump over the barrier. They just stood or lay around, waiting for the shocks to stop. A third group of dogs, which had never experienced shocks, quickly learned to jump the barrier.

Learned helplessness

Seligman concluded that the uncontrollable shocks had produced 'learned helplessness' in the second group of dogs;

they had learned that they could not control of the shocks, whatever they did, so why bother to do anything? Even when they took the barrier away and put food on the other side, the dogs did not bother to move. As Seligman wrote:

> When an experimenter goes to the home cage and attempts to remove a non-helpless dog, it does not comply eagerly; it barks, runs to the back of the cage and resists handling. In contrast, helpless dogs seem to wilt; they passively sink to the bottom of the cage, occasionally even rolling over and adopting a submissive posture; they do not resist.

People too?

Seligman and Miller found similar effects with people. In one experiment they asked people to do mental arithmetic while bombarding them with distracting noise. When some of them found they could turn off the noise, their performance improved, even though they often did not bother to turn it off. The point was that they knew they could turn it off; so they no longer felt helpless.

The researchers worked also with depressed people, and noticed that they sometimes showed the same sort of behaviour as the helpless dogs: weariness, sleeplessness, foreboding of disaster, mental numbness and so on. They made two suggestions: 1. some of the characteristics of depression are the effect of learned helplessness, and 2. the depressed people *believed* they were helpless.

Miller and Seligman suggested they adopt 'a depressive explanatory style' – beliefs such as 'The problem is that I am incompetent. I'll never be any use. I'm hopeless at everything.' Because they *believe* they are helpless, they are even more likely to get depressed.

They found that depressed patients in the hospital were more likely to give this sort of explanation than schizophrenics or normal medical students. Also, ordinary college students who got grades lower than they had hoped for – a B instead of an A, or a D instead of a C, were merely disappointed, but depressive students adopted a depressive explanatory style.

People are likely to succumb to 'hopelessness depression' if highly desirable things do not happen, or if highly unpleasant things do happen, and there is nothing that they can do about it.

Varieties of helplessness

Suppose a group of people are exposed to uncontrollable noise, but they are told that it is controllable. They cannot find out how, and may come to believe either that it really is uncontrollable, or that they lack the ability to control it.

The researchers went on to describe universal and personal helplessness. Suppose a child contracts leukaemia, and his father does everything he can to save the boy's life. Nothing helps, and he comes to believe there is nothing he can do, and nor can anyone else. He finally gives up, and shows signs of behavioural helplessness and depression. This is *universal helplessness*.

Suppose a student tries hard at mathematics, studies endlessly, takes extra courses, hires tutors, but nothing helps; she still fails her exams. She comes to believe she is stupid and gives up – and any mathematical question from estimating shopping bills to filling in a tax return will always be a nightmare. This is *personal helplessness*.

Conclusion

One ramification, as Miller and Seligman point out, is that people who fail in exams or in business, while others succeed, will acquire lower self-esteem than those who think that success is just a matter of luck. Also, a poor student who fails an exam that others pass will have lower self-esteem than if the others fail as well, for then he will think that the results were out of anyone's control.

CAN YOU LISTEN WITH YOUR EYES?

THE IMPORTANCE OF LIP-READING

1976

THE STUDY

RESEARCHERS:
Harry McGurk and
John MacDonald

SUBJECT AREA:
Perception

CONCLUSION:
We listen with
our eyes as well
as our ears.

Lip-reading sometimes makes you hear the wrong thing. When you talk to someone on the phone you have to rely on sound alone, but when you are speaking face to face you probably notice the other person's lips as you hear the voice. Lip-reading is helpful to most people, especially those whose hearing is impaired; indeed profoundly deaf people rely on lip-reading.

Harry McGurk noticed, however, one curious area of speech in which lip-reading actually hinders hearing. He saw a film of a young woman speaking to camera. She was saying 'ba . . . ba' but the sound of this had been put exactly into sync with the vision of her lips saying 'ga . . . ga.'

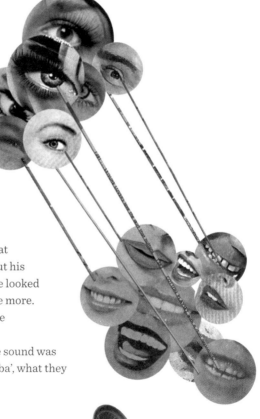

What do you think you would hear? What McGurk heard was 'da . . . da' – until he shut his eyes, when he heard 'ba . . . ba', but when he looked at the screen again he heard 'da . . . da' once more. Colleagues working with him had the same experiences.

When the process was reversed, and the sound was 'ga . . . ga' while the lips were saying 'ba . . . ba', what they heard was 'bagba' or 'gaba'.

Intrigued by these curious observations, McGurk decided to investigate further, using some clever lab experiments. He set out to confirm and generalize the discovery, by filming in close-up a woman saying 'ba . . . ba' three times; then 'ga . . . ga', followed by 'pa . . . pa', and finally 'ka . . . ka' each three times in a row. He carefully edited the film to make four separate recordings, as shown below.

Then he showed his edited film to 103 people: 21 preschool

Recording	1	2	3	4
Voice	ba . . . ba	ga . . . ga	pa . . . pa	ka . . . ka
Lips	ga . . . ga	ba . . . ba	ka . . . ka	pa . . . pa

children, 3 or 4 years old, 28 primary-school children, 7 or 8 years old, and 54 adults, mostly male. Each one watched the film alone, and said what they heard; then listened to the sound without seeing the lips, and said what they had heard.

The results were intriguing. Without the distraction of the lips, hearing was accurate: 91 per cent correct for the young children, 97 per cent for the older children, and 99 per cent for the adults.

When they watched the lips while listening, they heard the 'wrong' syllables 59 per cent, 52 per cent, and 92 per cent of the time.

He defined a 'fused' response as one where information from sound and lips was transformed into a new sound, different from either component; for example 'ba . . . ba' and 'ga . . . ga' turning into 'da . . . da'. When the sound and lips produced a modified version of one or the other – for example 'ga . . . ga' and 'ba . . . ba' turning into 'bagba' – he called it a 'combination'.

First of all, the results show that a majority of people experience closely similar effects: 98 per cent of adults heard the ba/ga combination as da and 81 per cent of adults heard pa/ka as ta. The children clearly relied more on hearing than on sight, but nevertheless more than 50 per cent of them heard the same fused results.

Adults were more influenced by the lips, and when they relied on one sense it was sight, whereas for the children it was sound.

Conclusion

McGurk points out that for hearing, vowels carry information for the consonants that immediately precede them, and concluded tentatively:

> *If we speculate that the acoustic waveform for 'ba' contains features in common with that for 'da' but not with 'ga,' then a tentative explanation for one set of the above illusions is suggested. Thus in a 'ba' voice 'ga' lips presentation there is visual information for 'ga' and 'da' and auditory information with features common to 'da' and 'ba.' By responding to the common information in both modalities, a subject would arrive at the unifying percept 'da'.*

These experiments remind us how much we – especially adults – rely on vision and lip-reading without realizing it, and should serve as a warning that we may often be confused or fooled by films or videos in which the sound recording is less than perfect.

1978

THE STUDY

RESEARCHER:
Edoardo Bisiach

SUBJECT AREA:
Perception

CONCLUSION:
Brain damage can
lead to a one-sided
view of the world.

HOW CAN YOU LOSE HALF THE WORLD?

HEMIFIELD AND UNILATERAL NEGLECT

Some people can apparently see only half the world in front of them. After a stroke, many people are left paralysed down one side of their bodies, or unable to speak properly, but a few have hemifield neglect, or unilateral neglect. This means that they do not seem to admit the existence of one side of their field of view.

If the damage is to the right side of the brain (most common), the left-hand side of the world seems to disappear. Men with unilateral neglect typically shave only the right side of their faces, and women make up their right side only. They eat only food on the right side of their plates; someone else has to turn the plate round so they can finish the meal. When asked to draw a picture, they will squash everything on to the right side. So a clock face may show only the right side, or the numbers may all be there, pushed over to the right, while a flower may have all the petals on one side.

Patients sometimes bump into objects, or door frames, with their left side, because they neglect them. What is so curious about this is that they have not really lost the vision of the left field. The information comes in, but they cannot process it. It seems as though they simply neglect it, or do not have their attention drawn to it.

Patients asked to read a word may read only the right half of the word and make the rest up. So invited to read the word PEANUT they may say 'nut' or 'walnut'. If you shake the left hand of such a patient and ask what it is, he may answer 'It's a hand'. But when asked whose hand he may say 'I don't know. It's not mine; it must be yours.' So the brain confabulates, or

makes up a story to fit what he sees as the facts.

Other experiments have shown that the right hemisphere can take in emotional messages, without being able to explain them. Marshall and Halligan showed patients a picture of two houses that were more-or-less identical, except that one had smoke and flames pouring out of the left-hand side. The patients said the houses were identical, but when asked which house they would rather live in they chose the non-burning one. They had clearly taken in the emotional message of one house on fire, though they had neglected to mention it to their vision system.

Bisiach showed that the neglect is deeper than just in vision, with an elegant demonstration. He works with patients in Milan, Italy, where everyone knows the spectacular *duomo*, or cathedral, and the grand square or piazza in front of it.

First he asked them to imagine themselves standing facing the *duomo,* and to describe the scene. They described all the buildings on the right-hand side of the piazza, but none on the left. Then he asked them to imagine standing with their backs to the *duomo,* and sure enough they described all the buildings on the other side of the piazza. Therefore they had the information about all the buildings, but from any one viewpoint ignored those on the left. What is more curious is that they did this not while standing in the piazza, but while imagining it; so clearly this one-sided view of the world was not confined to vision, but affected every part of their imagery. Presumably the views of the whole square had been stored in memory before the stroke, but only one side could be retrieved afterwards.

CHAPTER 6: Into consciousness: 1981–

Until the 1980s the word 'consciousness' was barely admitted in scientific discussions of the mind. How could anyone investigate consciousness? What is more, when the subject did creep in, psychologists had to confront 'the hard problem' – that mind and body seem separate, but must be related, or may even be the same thing. It may feel as though there is an 'I' inside, looking out through the eyes to see the world, but we know this is not the case.

Instead there is just an enormous mass of neurons, connected in billions of ways, processing information. And it was this bundle of pathways that scientists now began to investigate, through neuroscience experiments on such areas as free will and facial recognition, to synaesthesia and extrasensory perception.

1983

THE STUDY

RESEARCHERS:

Benjamin Libet, Curtis A Gleason, Elwood W Wright, and Dennis K Pearl

SUBJECT AREA:

Consciousness

CONCLUSION:

Free will may be a myth, but we are still responsible for our actions.

ARE YOU REALLY IN CONTROL?

THE NEUROSCIENCE OF FREE WILL

We all think we have conscious control over our actions, but is it true? In the 1980s, American neuropsychologist Benjamin Libet and his colleagues studied five right-handed college students, who sat in a partially reclining position on a lounger with their right arms out in front of them.

When they were comfortable, the trial began with a get-ready tone, at which they were instructed to spend the next second or two relaxing the muscles in the head, neck and forearm. Then, whenever they felt like doing so, they were to perform a quick, abrupt flip of the fingers or the wrist, and to do so spontaneously: 'to let the urge to act appear on its own at any time without any preplanning or concentration on when to act'. In other words they should flip their wrists whenever they felt like it, of their own free will, and do so 40 times.

Meanwhile, the researchers wanted to measure three things:

1. the time at which the movement began; this was recorded by electrodes on the forearm;

2. the onset of the 'Readiness Potential', which is a negative potential shift that slowly builds up a second or more before the action. The command from the brain goes to the muscles in the wrist shortly before they move. The Readiness Potential is the preparation for that command, and they measured it using electrodes on the scalp;

3. The moment of decision – 'the appearance of . . . conscious awareness of 'wanting' to perform a given self-initiated movement.' But this could only be subjective – only the subject could know when it happened. How could anyone possibly measure it?

The moment of decision

If the subjects were asked to shout 'Now', there would be a delay before the shout came out – so that would not work – and reflex time would also delay any mechanical action, such as pressing a button.

So what the researchers did was to put a screen in front of the subject and arrange for a spot of light to move around it in a circle about once every 2.5 seconds, like a hand on a clock face. The screen was marked with radial lines and numbers 1–12, as they appear on a clock face. The actual time taken for the spot to move from one number to the next was therefore about 43 milliseconds.

As the subjects decided to move their wrists, they called out the 'time' shown by the spot. This turned out to be highly reliable; subjects were consistently precise when asked to call the times of slight shocks delivered (at random intervals) to the back of the hand, and the small biases they displayed in this were used to correct the reported times for their decisions.

Readiness potential

The results showed a considerable range of times, but on average the Readiness Potential started about one second (1,000 ms) before the muscles

moved. The decision to act also preceded the actual movement. In every single one of several hundred trials, however, the decision came well after the onset of the Readiness Potential. The average difference was about 350 ms.

In other words the brain initiated the action about a third of a second before the subject 'decided' to act.

Libet and his colleagues wrote that this study:

> ... invites the extrapolation that other relatively 'spontaneous' voluntary acts, performed without conscious deliberation or planning, may also be initiated by cerebral activities proceeding unconsciously. These considerations would appear to introduce certain constraints on the potential of the individual for exerting conscious initiation and control over his voluntary acts.

Libet's results suggest that our conscious decisions may not be the cause of our actions; it's as though we do something spontaneously and then afterwards decide that we meant to do it. They even suggest that we may have no free will.

In 1985 Libet reported further experiments in which subjects had been instructed to veto the action after taking the decision to act. This time the muscles did not move. In other words, we do have time to exercise the veto, and so stop an action before it happens.

Conclusions

Libet's conclusions noted that it was:

> ... important to emphasize that the present experimental findings and analysis do not exclude the potential for 'philosophically real' individual responsibility and free will. Although the volitional

*process may be initiated by unconscious cerebral
activities, conscious control of the actual motor
performance of voluntary acts definitely remains
possible. The findings should therefore be taken
not as being antagonistic to free will but rather as
affecting the view of how free will might operate. The
concept of conscious veto or blockade of the motor
performance of specific intentions to act is in general
accord with certain religious and humanistic views
of ethical behaviour and individual responsibility.
'Self-control' of the acting out of one's intentions is
commonly advocated; in the present terms this would
operate by conscious selection or control of whether the
unconsciously initiated final volitional process will be
implemented in action. Many ethical strictures, such
as most of the Ten Commandments, are injunctions
not to act in certain ways.*

1984

THE STUDY

RESEARCHERS:
Diane C Berry and
Donald E Broadbent

SUBJECT AREA:
Cognition, decision-
making

CONCLUSION:
Practice, training and
thinking aloud is the
best combination.

DOES PRACTICE MAKE PERFECT?

'THE SUGAR FACTORY TASK'

After you have solved a problem, can you always explain how you did it? Berry and Broadbent wanted to investigate how people tackle complicated mental tasks. Does their performance improve with practice, or with training? And can they afterwards explain their methods?

This is a simplified account of one set of their experiments.

The sugar factory

They set up a computer simulation about managing an imaginary sugar factory. The problem appeared to be simple. The factory started with 600 workers producing 6,000 tons of sugar, and the subjects' task was to get sugar production up to 9,000 tons, and if possible keep it there for their entire run, by varying the number of workers in the factory.

In fact the computer was following a deceitful algorithm, but the subjects did not know this, and had to operate by guesswork and intuition.

The difficulties

The computer's algorithm meant that a workforce of say 800 would not always produce the same amount of sugar. This meant that the subjects had to be in control all the time; even if they hit 9,000 tons early on, putting in the same workforce would almost always change the output.

In each run they could make only a fixed number of 'tries' or key presses; their score was the number of tries after which production was between 8,000 and 10,000 tons. If they had chosen workforce numbers completely at random, they would have scored 3.4. If they did better than this they must have learned something about how to control production. Do you think they would do better than this? And would they improve with practice?

There were five groups of subjects. The first group, A, had only one run of 30 tries. The second group B had two runs of 30 tries, one after the other. The third group, C, had two runs of 20 tries, but after the first run they were given careful and explicit training in how to tackle the problem. The fourth group, D, were given no training, but encouraged to think aloud while they were doing the second run, in the hope of explaining what they were doing. The fifth group, E, were trained after the first run, and encouraged to think aloud while they were doing the second run.

The results

The average scores for Groups A and B are shown in the table. On average the subjects did much better than chance (3.4). Clearly they improved with practice, since Group B scored almost twice as much in their second run; so they must have learned something about how to solve the problem.

group	Score in 30 tries (max 30)	
	Run 1	Run 2
A	8.7	-
B	8.6	16.2

Explaining how they did it

After finishing their runs, subjects were asked to fill in questionnaires about how they had tackled the problem.

These questionnaires were then assessed and marked on a scale of 1 (bad) to 5 (good). Both groups A and B scored only 1.7 out of 5. In other words they could not explain what they had done. Group B were not significantly better than Group A, even though they had greatly improved at performing the task. What is more, subjects who had not even done the task scored 1.6 on the questionnaire, which was almost as good as those who had.

The subjects must have learned something, but they could not put it into words. Many claimed during their debriefing interviews that they were operating on the basis of 'some sort of intuition', making responses because they 'felt right'.

The results for groups C, D and E were even more interesting The scores are lower because the subjects had 20 tries instead of 30, but again they show that practice improved production, since the scores in run 2 were all higher than those in run 1. Training, however, seemed to have almost no effect on Group C, since their score in run 2 was hardly any better than Group D's.

The training did, however, have a spectacular effect on their ability to answer questions: Groups C and E scored roughly twice as much on the questionnaire as Groups A, B or D; so they did understand how they were meant to tackle the task.

Thinking aloud by itself did not have much effect either on performance or on answering questions, but when combined with the training it produced a spectacular increase during the second run.

Conclusions

1. Questionnaires cannot assess a person's performance.
2. Verbal training may not improve performance.
3. Even though people may get better at a task with practice, they may not be able to explain why.

Group	Score in 20 tries		Questionnaire
	Run 1	Run 2	
C (trained)	4.7	7.0	3.6
D (thinking aloud)	4.5	6.7	1.6
E (trained and thinking aloud)	5.2	13.3	3.4

Some people think of intuition as a mysterious force or inexplicable ability, but this experiment shows that it is perfectly normal to be able to learn a skill without knowing what you have learned. When you sense something wrong, or when you make a choice without knowing why, you are using just this kind of intuition.

HOW DO AUTISTIC CHILDREN SEE THE WORLD?

THE THEORY OF MIND

1985

THE STUDY

RESEARCHERS:
Simon Baron-Cohen,
Alan M Leslie and Uta
Frith

SUBJECT AREA:
Developmental
psychology

CONCLUSION:
Autistic children
cannot interpret
others' mental states.

Autism is rare; it affects about four children in 10,000. Autistic children are unusual in many ways, but in particular they are challenged by poor communication, both verbal and non-verbal. This is one of the main reasons why they have trouble in coping with the social environment, and they do not develop social relationships.

Baron-Cohen and his colleagues wondered whether they can understand that other people want, feel or believe things, which is called having a 'theory of mind (TOM)'. In most children this begins to appear when they are three or four. Autistic children, even those with high IQs, do not enjoy pretend play. So the researchers predicted that autistic children would not have a theory of mind.

They compared 20 autistic children with 14 children with Down's Syndrome and 27 non-autistic preschool children aged between 3.5 and 6. The average mental age of the autistic children was higher than that of both the Down's group and the non–special needs group. The average IQs were 82 for the autistic group and 64 for the Down's group.

The experiment

With each of the children in turn they acted out a little story with two dolls, Sally and Anne. First they named the dolls, and asked the children which was Sally and which was Anne. All 61 children got this right.

Then they played a game, using the dolls. Sally put a marble into her basket. Then she went away, and Anne took the marble and hid it in her box. When Sally came back, the experimenter asked the critical Belief Question: 'where will Sally look for her marble?' If the children point to the basket, then they pass the belief question by appreciating that Sally now has a false belief. If, however, they point to the box, then they fail the question. They know where the marble has been hidden, but cannot appreciate that Sally does not know.

They then repeated the whole procedure, but this time the marble ended in the experimenter's pocket.

After each scene, the experimenter asked two more crucial questions: the 'reality' question 'Where is the marble really?' and the memory question 'Where was the marble in the beginning?' All the children, without exception, got these right; they knew where the marble was now, and they remembered where it had started.

When asked 'Where will Sally look for her marble?' the children varied. Among non–special needs children, 85 per cent got it right – they pointed to her basket – and so did 86 per cent of the Down's children, but only 20 per cent of the autistic children did so.

The four autistic children who got the answer right did not appear to be much different from the others in the group; they had average ages and mental ages. Every single child answered the control questions correctly; so they all understood what was going on; they knew (and believed) that the marble was put somewhere else after Sally left.

The non–special needs and Down's children answered the belief question by pointing to Sally's basket. The researchers concluded that:

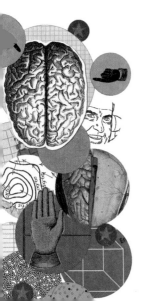

*...they must have appreciated that their own knowledge
of where the marble actually was, and the knowledge
that could be attributed to the doll, were different. That
is, they predicted the doll's behaviour on the basis of the
doll's belief.*

*The autistic group, on the other hand, answered by
pointing consistently to where the marble really was.
They did not merely point to a 'wrong' location, but
rather to the actual location of the marble.... We
therefore conclude that the autistic children did not
appreciate the difference between their own and the
doll's knowledge.*

*Our results strongly support the hypothesis that
autistic children as a group fail to employ a theory
of mind. We explain this as an inability to represent
mental states. As a result of this, autistic subjects
are unable to impute beliefs to others and are thus
at a grave disadvantage when having to predict the
behaviour of other people. Thus we have demonstrated
a cognitive deficit that is largely independent of general
intellectual level and has the potential to explain both
lack of pretend play and social impairment by virtue of
a circumscribed cognitive failure.*

On the other hand, the researchers thought that perhaps
the four autistic children who did get the belief question
right – and they all did so in both versions of the story –
may employ a theory of mind, might be able to take part in
pretend play and might have less trouble in forming social
relationships.

The Sally-Anne test has been widely used as a way to study
theory of mind in children and its relationship to social
interaction and empathy.

1988

THE STUDY

RESEARCHER:

Randolph C Byrd

SUBJECT AREA:

Social psychology

CONCLUSION:

Byrd's data seemed
to show prayer had a
beneficial effect.

CAN PRAYER HELP HEAL THE SICK?

STUDIES ON INTERCESSORY PRAYER

If you became seriously ill, would you like other people to pray for you? In 1872, Francis Galton reported on the effectiveness of prayer on clergy, and found no positive effects. He also pointed out that in England, even though thousands of people prayed each Sunday for the health of the royal family, none of the kings or queens had actually lived significantly longer than their prominent contemporaries.

More than a century later, Randolph Byrd set out to investigate. In the coronary care unit at San Francisco General Hospital he invited 450 patients to consent to being prayed for, while they were in the hospital; 393 agreed.

He divided the patients randomly into two groups, 192 to get intercessory prayer and 201 not to be prayed for. Neither he, nor the patients, nor doctors and staff knew who was in which group.

The intercessory prayers

The intercessors were all 'born-again Christians ... with an active Christian life as manifested by daily devotional prayer and active Christian Fellowship with a local church'. Each patient in group 1 was allotted between three and seven intercessors, who were given the patient's first name, diagnosis and general condition.

The prayer was done outside the hospital every day until the patient was discharged. 'Each intercessor was asked to pray daily for a rapid recovery and for prevention of complications and death'.

The hospital record provided details of no less than 30 different conditions that affected these patients, but overall there was no significant difference between the two groups when they were admitted to hospital.

The hospital course after entry 'was considered to be *good* if . . . events occurred that only minimally increased the patient's morbidity or risk of death. The course was considered *intermediate* if there were higher levels of morbidity and a moderate risk of death. The course of patients who had the highest morbidity and risk of death, or who died during the study was graded as *bad*.'

The results

In the prayer group 85 per cent of the patients were considered to have a *good* hospital course, as opposed to 73 per cent in the control group. An *intermediate* grade was given in 1 per cent of the prayer group, and 5 per cent of the controls. A *bad* hospital cause was observed in 14 per cent of the prayer group, and 22 per cent of the controls.

Conclusions

Byrd concludes that the prayer group 'had less congestive heart failure, required less diuretic and antibiotic therapy, had fewer episodes of pneumonia, had fewer cardiac arrests and were less frequently intubated and ventilated . . .' So 'the prayer group had an overall better outcome. . . . Based on thus data there seem to be an effect, and that effect was presumed to be beneficial'.

On the other hand, some reviewers were sceptical, on the grounds that there were positive outcomes in only six of the

30 different conditions affecting the patients, and one critic compared Byrd's results with the 'sharpshooter fallacy' – 'searching through the data until a significant effect is found, then drawing the bull's-eye.'

Many later experiments, attempting to reproduce Byrd's results, have produced either very little positive evidence, or none. In 2006 Herbert Benson reported the enormous STEP project (Study of the Therapeutic Effects of Intercessory Prayer) with 1,802 coronary artery bypass patients.

They were divided into three groups: Group A (604 patients) were told that they might or might not be prayed for – and in fact were prayed for. Group B (597) were also told that they might or might not be prayed for – and in fact were not prayed for. Group C (601) were told that they would be prayed for, and were. Prayer started the day before their operations and continued for 14 days.

Quality of hospital course		
Score	Prayer group (192 patients)	Control group (201 patients)
Good	163	147
Intermediate	2	10
Bad	27	44

Benson found that within a month major complications and sometimes death happened to 52 per cent of Group A, 51 per cent of Group B and 59 per cent of Group C. In other words people who knew that prayers were being said for them actually came off worse than the others. Perhaps this was 'performance anxiety'; they were seriously stressed by thinking they might fail to respond to the prayers.

DO YOU NEVER FORGET A FACE?

THE EFFECTS OF PROSOPAGNOSIA AFTER A STROKE

RESEARCHERS:
Jane E Mcneil
and Elizabeth K
Warrington

SUBJECT AREA:
Social psychology

CONCLUSION:
Sometimes sheep are
easier to recognize
than humans.

Can you imagine being able to recognize sheep more easily than humans? After a stroke, some people develop prosopagnosia (also known as 'face blindness'), a condition in which people are unable to recognize other people's faces. A few people also suffer prosopagnosia all their lives. The lack of recognition sometimes extends to other things. There was a prosopagnosic bird-watcher who could no longer recognize birds, a farmer who could no longer recognize his own cows, another who could recognize his cows and dogs, but not human faces and so on. McNeil and Warrington worked with a patient, W J, who after a series of strokes had acquired severe prosopagnosia, and could not recognize human faces.

When they tested him, W J was able to identify only two out of 12 well-known faces, and even then he had to work them out carefully. He could not judge age, sex or expression on faces in photographs. On the other hand he was 95 per cent accurate in naming famous buildings, breeds of dog, makes of car and flowers.

He also claimed that he could recognize his sheep by their faces.

Sebastian

Mr Pickles

Lady

Recognizing sheep?

For two years he had owned a flock of sheep, which were identified by number tags in their ears. When they showed him close-up photographs of 16 of his sheep (with ear tags omitted from the pictures) he was able to identify eight of them, but clearly knew some of the others, as in several cases he would say things like, 'I know that sheep very well; she's the one that had three lambs last year, but I can't remember her number.' Clearly he was better at recognizing the faces of sheep than of humans.

In order to avoid the problem of having to remember numbers, the researchers arranged a different recognition test. They showed, at three-second intervals, eight photographs of sheep's faces, asking only whether or not they were pleasant sheep. Then they showed 16 photographs, which were the same eight plus eight different sheep, but mixed up in a random order, and asked in each case whether the sheep in the photograph was one of the first eight, or not. They gave the same test to two other people with flocks of sheep and five other farmers, who commented that the sheep all looked the same, and were incredibly difficult to recognize.

W J was hopeless with human faces; he was probably guessing, since he scored just 50 per cent, which is the score you would expect by chance. Clearly, however, he was much better than the others at recognizing sheep.

As a further test, they went through the same procedure again, but using photographs of a different breed of sheep,

	W J	Farmers	Sheep-owners
	Accuracy of recognition (per cent)		
Familiar sheep	87	66	59
Unfamiliar sheep	81	69	63
Human faces	50	89	100

with which W J was not familiar. The results were similar, though less dramatic.

The researchers then tried another test. They showed six photographs of faces of unfamiliar sheep, and gave each one a plausible name. Then they showed the photographs in random order and asked the subjects to provide the correct name when the photograph appeared. They did the same

	WJ	Farmers	Sheep-owners
	Accuracy of recognition (per cent)		
Human faces	23	71	78
Sheep	57	41	55

thing with six human faces and names. Once again, W J was poor with human faces, but outclassed the controls when it came to sheep.

The researchers were baffled by W J. He had bought the sheep after his strokes, and therefore had learned to recognize their faces at the same time as he was unable to recognize human faces. They discuss how he might have done this:

> *It is possible that he developed a sheep 'prototype,' which enables the effective encoding of sheep facial features. What is quite surprising, however, is the extent to which his abilities appear to generalize to other visually dissimilar breeds of sheep. Perhaps the more remarkable finding is that W J has been totally unable to overcome his prosopagnosia.... He seems unable to utilize the sorts of strategies he has learned to use for sheep.*

1994

THE STUDY

RESEARCHERS:
Daryl J Bemm and
Charles Honorton

SUBJECT AREA:
Perception

CONCLUSION:
Honorton's tests show
that mind-reading
might be possible,
but his results have
yet to be matched.

IS THERE ANY SENSE IN ESP?

FINDING EVIDENCE FOR EXTRASENSORY PERCEPTION

Daryl J Bemm and Charles Honorton knew they were fighting an uphill battle with this research. Most academic psychologists don't think paranormal phenomena exists at all. And even believers have no idea how it might work.

Extrasensory Perception (ESP)

The first serious research into ESP was conducted in the 1930s at Duke University in North Carolina by J B Rhine and his wife Louisa. The Rhines set out to investigate various apparently paranormal phenomena. In particular Rhine used a special pack of cards designed by a colleague, Karl Zener.

There were 25 cards in the pack, five of each type. The pack was shuffled and cut, and then a subject had to guess each card before it was dealt. By pure chance you should guess right one time in five, or 20 per cent. Some of Rhine's subjects achieved much higher scores, but the effects were hard to replicate, and there may have been 'sensory leakage', (where an experimenter involuntarily reveals the answer) or even cheating. Nevertheless, in 1934 Rhine wrote a book called *Extra-Sensory Perception*, which was where the term ESP came from.

Ganzfeld and autoganzfeld

Bemm and Honorton's basic plan was that a 'sender' should watch a short film clip – the 'target' – and try to send ideas and images from the film to a 'receiver.' Both sender and receiver were isolated, and no contact was possible between them.

After half an hour, an experimenter went into the receiver's room and showed four possible film clips. The receiver then had to guess the target on the basis of which one most closely resembled the ideas and images that had arrived during that half hour.

There had been suggestions that psychic activity was more likely to occur during relaxation and meditation, so Honorton had invented a method that he called the *Ganzfeld* (German for 'entire field'). The receiver lay comfortably on a reclining chair. White noise, like waves on a sea shore, was played into their headphones. Over the eyes were half ping-pong balls, lit with warm red light. These conditions were meant to put the receiver in an ideal state to receive incoming messages from the sender, which would be telepathy, or to see the film clip directly, which would be clairvoyance.

While the sender was 'sending,' the receiver talked continuously about the ideas and images that turned up, and all this was recorded for later analysis.

People had argued over the original Ganzfeld experiments; there might have been sensory leakage or cheating. Honorton set up the elaborate autoganzfeld in order to try to silence the critics, since the automatic procedure should eliminate any problems. He used a computer, which chose the film clip from a bank of 80 clips, and showed it repeatedly to the sender.

At the end of the session an experimenter removed the ping-pong balls, switched off red light and white noise, and switched on a TV set, where the computer showed, in random order, the film clip, along with three others, for the receiver to guess which had been the target. They were allowed to watch the clips and adjust the ratings as often as they liked. Their final ratings were saved on the computer, and then the sender came in to discuss the results. The experimenter who sat with the receiver did not know until this point what the target was. With his elaborate security arrangements, Honorton reckoned he had prevented both sensory leakage and fraud.

The results

By chance alone they should have got it right a quarter of the time, since there were four possible clips, and any of them could have been the target. Thus any score significantly above 25 per cent could count as evidence for psychic phenomena.

This large study had 240 participants, most of whom were strong believers in ESP. They took part in 329 sessions, and scored 106 hits, which corresponds to a score of 32 per cent – much better than the expected 25 per cent.

In order to also see if artistic people are be better suited to psychic communication than the average the researchers recruited ten male and ten female students from the Juilliard School – eight music students, ten drama students and two dancers. This group did one session each, and achieved an extraordinary score of 50 per cent.

Conclusions

Bemm and Honorton believed that they had scientifically proved the existence of ESP. Their paper was one of the first paranormal papers accepted for publication by a mainstream psychology journal. Sadly, however, because of lack of funding, Honorton's lab was closed down before the study could be repeated, and Honorton himself died nine days before the paper was accepted for publication. No one else has been able to produce such positive results.

WHY CAN'T YOU ALWAYS SPOT THE DIFFERENCE?

THE PECULIAR PHENOMENON OF CHANGE BLINDNESS

1995

THE STUDY

RESEARCHERS:
Daniel J Simons and
Daniel T Levin

SUBJECT AREA:
Perception

CONCLUSION:
We sometimes fail
to see what's right in
front of our nose.

Sometimes it takes only the smallest distraction to make someone unaware of substantial changes in the scene they are looking at. 'Change blindness' was first reported by the English psychologist Susan Blackmore and her colleagues in 1995. They showed that when you look at two pictures showing almost the same scene, you are unlikely to notice a substantial change from one to the other, provided the two versions are separated by a flash frame, or a blank frame, or when they are in slightly different places on the screen. These experiments were all of two-dimensional pictures.

Later that same year, the American experimental psychologists Simons and Levin wanted to try the same test in three dimensions using short films. In one film an actor walked through an empty classroom and sat in a chair. The footage cut to a close up and a different actor completed the action. Even though the actors were easy to tell apart only 33 per cent of the 40 participants reported noticing the change.

In the real world

Simons and Levin decided to take this idea into the real world, and see whether change blindness would still work when the participant was actively engaged with an experimenter. One experimenter waited on the campus of Cornell University holding a map, and then approached an unsuspecting pedestrian to ask for directions to the library.

After the experimenter and the pedestrian had been talking for 10 or 15 seconds, two other experimenters carrying a door walked towards them along the pavement, and rudely pushed their way between them.

As the door passed, the first experimenter grabbed the back of the door and walked on, while one of the others let go of the door, stayed behind and carried on asking directions.

The second experimenter had a copy of the same map, but was dressed in different clothes. When the directions were complete the experimenter said 'We're doing a study as part of the psychology department . . . of the sorts of things people pay attention to in the real world. Did you notice anything unusual at all when that door passed by a minute ago?'

Any subjects who had not noticed the change were then asked directly 'Did you notice that I'm not the same person who approached you to ask for directions?'

There were 15 pedestrians in this experiment, male and female, ranging in age from 20 to 65. When asked whether they had noticed anything unusual, most of them said they thought the people with the door were rude, but eight of them – more than half – had not noticed the switch. They simply carried on the conversation, and were surprised to learn that the direction-seeker had been replaced by someone else in mid flow. Interestingly, those who did notice the change were all in the same age range (20–30) as the experimenters; older people were less likely to notice. The researchers speculate that this might be because the younger pedestrians, recognizing people of their own age group (the in-group) were more likely to expend effort in noting their features.

Experiment 2

In order to test this idea, they carried out the same procedure again, tackling unsuspecting passers-by, but this time the experimenters dressed as builders – there was a building site nearby – and wore strikingly different clothes.

They approached only young (20–30) pedestrians, and this time only four out of 12 noticed the switch.

Even though the two experimenters wore strikingly different clothes, the pedestrians probably saw them as 'builders' – an out-group – and therefore not worth close inspection. The researchers wrote 'One subject said that she had just seen a construction worker and had not coded the properties of the individual. . . . Even though the experimenter was the centre of attention, she did not code the visual details and compare them across views. Instead, she formed a representation of the category.'

Simons and Levin point out that these experiments build on the work of Loftus (page 119) and Bartlett (page 34), but show in addition that people often do not notice changes in the scene even when they are actively engaged and the change is to the central object in the scene. After hearing about the experiment, 50 introductory psychology students all insisted that they would have spotted the substitution. This has been called 'change-blindness blindness'.

We certainly don't expect to be fooled in this way – but we often are. These and many other experiments should make us wonder how much of what is going on around us we simply never see.

1998

THE STUDY

RESEARCHERS:
Marcello Costantini
and Patrick Haggard

SUBJECT AREA:
Perception

CONCLUSION:
We can sometimes
misperceive our own
bodies.

———————————

COULD YOU CONFUSE A FAKE HAND WITH YOUR OWN?

THE RUBBER HAND ILLUSION

Lay your hand on a table in front of you, with a fake hand (try using an inflated rubber glove) beside it in the same orientation. Hide your hand and get someone to stroke both the rubber hand and your own, at the same time and in the same way, and you may suddenly feel that the rubber hand is your hand. This illusion was first discovered by two psychiatrists from the University of Pittsburgh, Matthew Botvinick and Jonathan Cohen, in 1998.

Psychologists talk about 'body schema' and body image. Body schema is the model of your body that you can feel with your eyes shut; it allows you to walk around without bumping into obstacles, because you know where your limbs are; this is part of what's known as 'proprioception'.

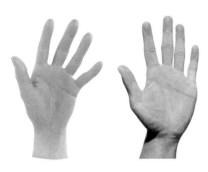

Your 'body image' is a conscious idea of your body, including what it looks like from the outside. Together with body schema, it forms a coherent base for self-consciousness. The American researchers, Marcello Costantini and Patrick Haggard, wanted to take the idea further and find out whether our experience of our body come mainly from the inside (schema) or from the outside (image)?

———

Proprioceptive drift

The participant sat at a table and put her arm on it, in front of the shoulder, with the hand laid flat, palm down. (There were 13 male and 13 female participants, with an average age of 28.) She could see the rubber hand, but not her own. The rubber hand was lined up with hers, and 30 centimetres (12 inches) away from it.

Her hand and the rubber hand were stroked exactly in sync and in the same place, with 1 mm paintbrushes, under computer control. Because she saw and felt the stroking, a typical participant was confused by the conflicting signals of sight and touch, and would say this made the rubber hand 'feel like my own hand.'

One consequence was that she thought her own unseen hand was closer to the rubber hand than it actually was. This is called 'proprioceptive drift,' because she felt she knew the position of her hand by proprioception – part of the body schema. Participants were asked to measure the distance between the rubber hand and where they felt their own hands to be, which provided the experimenters with a measure of the power of the illusion. In the strongest cases the participants felt as if their hands were a few centimetres closer to the rubber hand than they really were; this was the amount of proprioceptive drift.

The researchers investigated what happens as they varied the angles of the stroking and the hands. There were two groups of participants. To begin with they lined up the rubber hand precisely with the real hand, and stroked both down the back to the middle finger. This is the baseline condition.

In one group they manipulated the real hand, while in the second group they manipulated the rubber hand. They expected the illusion to disappear sooner in the second group, since you can detect a change of angle easily by sight, but not so easily by proprioception.

The first manipulation was to vary the angle at which the paintbrush stroked the hand. Next, they rotated the hand, but kept the stroking the same with respect to the hand, or in 'hand-centred space'. Finally they rotated the hand, while the stroking remained in the same direction as it had been in the baseline condition. There would be a mismatch if the participant felt the stroking in a hand-centred space, but no mismatch if she felt it in an external egocentric space.

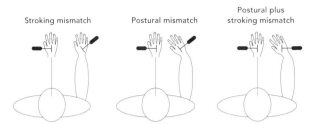

Stroking mismatch　　Postural mismatch　　Postural plus stroking mismatch

Keeping up the illusion

In the proprioceptive group – rotating the real hand – the illusion changed a little at 10 degrees, significantly more at 20 degrees and 30 degrees. In the visual group, however – rotating the rubber hand – even a 10 degrees mismatch destroyed the illusion altogether. In other words, changing the angle of the rubber hand, which the participant could see, produced a much greater effect than changing the position of the real hand.

In the first picture above, only the stroking is off line, relative to both the participant and the hand. In the second, the hand and the stroking are off line relative to the participant, but the stroking in not off line relative to the hand. In the third picture, the hand is off line, and the stroking is off line relative to the hand, although not relative to the observer.

Since this third condition gave much the most dramatic change in the RHI, the researchers concluded that the stroking is felt in a hand-centred space.

The researchers conclude that 'the brain maintains an internal body representation, with its own characteristic spatial organization based on proprioception. This representation uses a frame of reference based on the specific part of the body that is stimulated.' In other words, when your hand is stroked, you feel the sensation in hand-centred space, not body-centred space.

WHY CAN'T YOU TICKLE YOURSELF?

FINDING ANSWERS TO A TICKLISH QUESTION

2000
THE STUDY

RESEARCHERS:
Sarah-Jayne Blakemore, Daniel Wolpert and Chris Frith

SUBJECT AREA:
Neuropsychology

CONCLUSION:
There is a surprising link between ticklishness and schizophrenia.

We can easily tell the difference between sensations caused by our own movements and those caused by other things; the difference between pushing and being pushed is obvious. The researchers suggest this is because when we do something, the brain sends messages to the muscles to act, and at the same time provides advance warning, known as an 'efference copy,' that the relevant action is going to happen; so we are not surprised to see our arms go out to push. If we don't get that warning, on the other hand, we are surprised.

When you turn your head or your eyes to look at something, the warning means that you can work out where in the world is the thing you are looking at.

With both eyes open, try pressing gently with a finger on your eyelid near the outside corner of your eye. In the view from that eye, the world begins to swivel. This is because the brain has not received the warning that the eye was about to move, and can't compute the image it receives.

In normal, everyday movements therefore there is forward planning, which is backed up as the movement happens by further messages, confirming the movement happens as planned, or adjusting it if necessary. The forward planning and the confirming feedback can be used to damp down, or attenuate, the sensations caused by the movement.

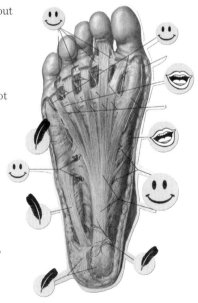

Tickling yourself

Tickling yourself does not really work. You can still feel it, but it is not very tickly. The researchers suggested that the forward planning warns you not only that there is going to be movement across your skin, but exactly when and where it will happen – and automatically damps down the sensation.

To test their hypothesis, the researchers asked 16 subjects to hold out their right hands for tickling, and to rate the ticklishness of a piece of soft foam moved 1.5 centimetres (0.6 inches) in a figure-of-eight pattern across the palm twice every second. The foam was attached to a robotic arm.

First the robot did all the action, which felt very tickly – 3.5 on the Tickle Rating Rank. Then the subjects moved the foam themselves, by using their left hands to move a knob on the arm of a second robot, which transferred the movement to the first; so the subject had complete control of the movement.

The clever part of the experiment was that the researchers were able to introduce variations, either by delaying the movement, so that it was just the same as that caused by the subject, but fractions of a second later, or by changing the direction of the movement, so that when the subject moved say north-south (N-S), the foam went a bit clockwise, through NE-SW to E-W.

The results

The subjects said that tickling themselves (via the robot arms) was much less tickly (about 2.1) than being tickled by the robot, but the sensations became gradually stronger as the self-tickling was progressively delayed or twisted. By the time the movement was delayed by 300 ms (nearly one third of a second), or skewed by 90 degrees from north-south to east-west, the tickling was almost as good as if the robot was doing it. These results strongly support the theory that when you try to tickle yourself, the sensation is damped down by the advance warning of your own movements. Without any delay or skewing, the ticklishness is reduced by nearly 50 per cent, but the more delay or skewing there is, the less accurate is the advance warning, and the more tickly it becomes.

Connection with schizophrenia

Lack of this forward planning and confirmation may possibly be involved in schizophrenia. A common symptom is hearing voices. This might be the result of internally generated voices or thoughts for which there are no warning messages. Another common symptom is called 'passivity phenomena.' For example schizophrenics may feel some of their own actions are caused by other people: 'my fingers pick up the pen, but I don't control them. What they do is nothing to do with me.' Again, that may be what it feels like if there is no advance warning.

Can there really be a connection between ticklishness and schizophrenia? To find out, the researchers tried tickling tests on patients with schizophrenia, bipolar affective disorder or depression, dividing them into two groups. The 15 patients of group A all had auditory hallucinations (hearing voices) and/or passivity experiences. The 23 patients of group B had neither of these symptoms. Group C comprised 15 non-patients.

All these people held out their right hands, and either were tickled by the experimenter or tickled themselves with the other hand. All those in groups B and C said that when they tickled themselves it was much less intense, tickly and pleasant. Patients in group A said that tickling themselves was just as effective as being tickled by the experimenter.

This suggests that hearing voices and passive experiences may well be associated with lack of that vital advance warning of movement.

THE STUDY

RESEARCHERS:
Researchers: V. S.
Ramachandran
and E. H. Hubbard

SUBJECT AREA:
Perception

CONCLUSION:
For some people
the senses are
all connected.

CAN YOU TASTE THE NUMBER 7?

THE EXTRAORDINARY EFFECTS OF SYNAESTHESIA

A small fraction of people, perhaps one in a thousand, experience curious mixtures of senses; they hear numbers as distinct musical tones, taste letters and see days of the week as coloured. This is called synaesthesia, often runs in families, is more common among women, left-handers, artists and poets.

Is it a genuine phenomenon, or just imagination?

The condition was first described by Francis Galton in 1880, but for more than a century, scientists and refused to take the idea seriously for a variety of reasons:

1. 'Synaesthetes' are just crazy. The phenomenon is simply the result of a hyperactive imagination.

2. They are just remembering childhood memories such as seeing coloured numbers in books or playing with coloured fridge magnets.

3. They are just engaging in vague tangential speech or just being metaphorical, just as you and I might say 'bitter cold' or 'mature cheese'.

4. They are 'potheads' or 'acid junkies' who have been on drugs. This idea is not entirely absurd, since LSD users often do report synaesthesia both during the high as well as long after.

Ramachandran ('Rama') and Hubbard took the claims more seriously, and decided to investigate. They used some elegant experiments to investigate whether synaesthesia depends on the vision system rather than imagination, or memory.

How synaesthetes see

They showed people displays of square 2s and 5s like the one on the right. Can you see a triangle of 2s within the display?

If you are not a synaesthete this may take several seconds, but if 2s and 5s are different colours for you (as in the display on the next page) then the triangle should pop out instantly. This is exactly what happened with the synesthetes. They could not have been making this up.

Synaesthetes say that a letter or numeral printed in the 'wrong' colour is ugly. 'Also they often report 'odd' or weird colours they cannot see in the real world but see only in association with numbers. We even saw a colour-blind subject recently who saw certain colours only upon seeing numbers.'

The researchers noted that colour processing in the brain, in both humans and monkeys, happens in an area called the fusiform gyrus, right next to the area in which visual letters and numbers are processed. The most common form of synesthesia is to see letters and numbers as coloured. They therefore propose that synesthesia is caused by cross-wiring in the brain between these two processes.

They further propose that since synaesthesia runs in families, 'a single gene mutation causes an excess of cross-connections or defective pruning of connections between different brain areas. Consequently, every time there is activation of neurons representing numbers, there may be a corresponding activation of colour neurons.'

Top-down influence

Rama and Hubbard showed synaesthetes the Roman numeral IV. They saw the colours for I and V when it looked like letters, but not the colour expected for the number four.

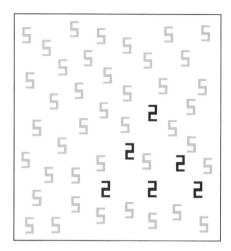

The implication of these observations is that synaesthesia can be modulated by top-down influence; there is clearly some processing before the colour appears.

Conclusion

At the end of a long, speculative paper, Rama and Hubbard write:

Synaesthesia has always been regarded as somewhat spooky. Even though it has been known for over 100 years, it has often been thought of as a curiosity ... our psychophysical experiments were the first to prove conclusively that synaesthesia is a genuine sensory phenomenon.

They speculate that studying synaesthesia may help us understand the neural basis of metaphor and creativity:

Perhaps the same mutation that causes cross-wiring in the fusiform, if expressed very diffusely, can lead to more extensive cross-wiring in their brains. [This could] explain the higher incidence of synaesthesia in artists, poets and novelists (whose brains may be more cross-wired, giving them greater opportunity for metaphors).

IS ASTRAL TRAVEL OUT OF THIS WORLD?

THE SCIENCE BEHIND OUT-OF-BODY EXPERIENCES

2007

THE STUDY

RESEARCHERS:
Bigna Lenggenhager,
Tej Tadi, Thomas
Metzinger
and Olaf Blanke

SUBJECT AREA:
Perception

CONCLUSION:
There is no conclusive
evidence to prove
out-of-body
experiences exist.

Apparently one person in ten has at least one out-of-body experience (OBE) during their lifetime. In typical OBEs, people feel that they have left their body and can see the world from a location outside it – often looking down from a position near the ceiling. OBEs can form a dramatic part of a near-death experience, but OBEs are far more common in people who are perfectly well, most often happening during deep relaxation. Occasionally they happen in scary situations like giving a lecture or appearing on stage.

Some people are terrified that they will not be able to return to their body, when in fact it is much harder to maintain the experience, and it usually lasts only a few seconds or a few minutes. Others enjoy the experience so much that they try to induce it, for example by hovering in the hypnagogic state just before falling asleep, or by taking drugs such as ketamine.

Allegedly Thomas Alva Edison used to get into this hypnagogic state deliberately while wrestling with invention problems. He would sit in a chair, holding a bucket and put a silver dollar on his head. When he nodded off, the dollar fell into the bucket and awoke his mind, while his body slept.

Psychological or paranormal?

The big question for OBEs is whether anything actually leaves the body during the experience. People of many cultures have theories about souls or spirits that can separate from the physical body, and even survive after death. One such is the doctrine of astral projection, according to which we may have 'subtle bodies' including an astral body that can project beyond its physical home and into the astral planes. Yet there is no reliable evidence for the existence of astral bodies or planes. Also many people who have OBEs claim to be able to see at a distance, but there is no good evidence that this is true either.

In 2002 a Swiss neurosurgeon discovered a spot in the brain where OBEs can be induced, and there was a burst of scientific research on OBEs. Some involved brain research; others used virtual reality, like this experiment by Bigna Lenggenhager and her colleagues in Zurich. They wanted to try to induce OBEs artificially, by using an extension of the rubber-hand illusion (see page 160), in which vision dominates proprioception. In order to do this, they invited participants to enter into a world of virtual reality.

Experiment A

The participant wore a head-mounted display unit (HMD), and stood in the middle of the room. A video camera was mounted on a tripod 2 metres (2.2 yards) behind, and the image of the participant's back was transmitted to the HMD. The result was that the participants could see a three-dimensional image of their own backs apparently standing 2 metres (2.2 yards) in front of them. An experimenter then stroked their backs for one minute, and the sensation of feeling their backs being stroked, while watching the same thing, induced the participants to believe that they were seeing themselves standing two metres away. When the virtual stroking was arranged to be out of sync with the actual stroking the effect was much reduced.

Immediately after the stroking had finished the participants were blindfolded and asked to move back to their original position. As predicted, they moved forward – toward where the virtual body had been. This 'proprioceptive drift' averaged 24 centimetres (9.5 inches), if the stroking had been in sync, but only half as much when it had not.

Experiments B & C

The experimenters then put a fake body in front of the camera, and stood the participants two metres away to the side. Then they stroked both the participant's body and the fake body. Participants therefore saw, apparently standing 2 metres (2.2 yards) in front of them, a fake body being stroked at the same time as their own backs. Provided that the stroking was exactly in sync, they came to feel that they were looking at themselves, as when they had been looking at the image of their own bodies. Furthermore when blindfolded, they stepped forward and showed if anything slightly more proprioceptive drift.

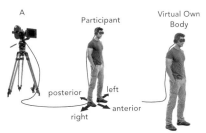

When the fake body was replaced by a box, however, the participants were no longer persuaded that it was their own body they were looking at, and showed virtually no drift.

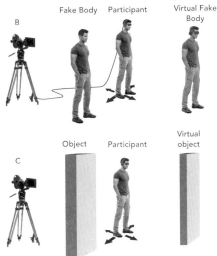

Conclusions

The researchers write: 'illusory self-localization to a position outside one's body shows that bodily self-consciousness and selfhood can be dissociated from one's physical body position.'

On the other hand they acknowledge that because the participants did not feel disembodied, and maintained their original perspective – as opposed for example to looking down on themselves from above – the experiments induced only some parts of a typical OBE.

Index

Glossary

chaining – reinforcing individual responses in a sequence to form a complex pattern of behaviour.

change blindness – a phenomenon that occurs when a change in scene is introduced and not noticed.

cognitive dissonance – mental stress caused by holding two contradictory beliefs at the same time, or by encountering information that contradicts an existing belief.

cognitive psychology – the study of mental processes such as attention, language use, memory, perception, creativity, and problem solving.

corpus callosum – a wide band of nerve fibers that connects the left and right sides of the brain and transfers information between them.

EEG – electroencephalogram, recording electrical activity along the scalp.

extrinsic reward – an expected reward for something done, that does not lead to greater satisfaction.

ingroup – a small exclusive group of people with a common interest.

Gestalt – an organized whole that is seen to be more than the sum of its parts.

heuristic – a shortcut method of solving problems, which may disregard some information, and may not give the right or best answer.

intrinsic reward – reward for a job that comes from satisfaction of a job well done, and a sense of achievement.

kinaesthesis – the ability to feel movements of the limbs and body.

operant conditioning – learning through reinforcements and punishments for particular actions.

outgroup – a group of people to which you do not belong.

proprioception – the sense of how the various parts of your body are positioned.

proprioceptive drift – the idea that your body or its parts have moved, or is in the wrong place.

reflex action – instinctive response to a stimulus.

saccade – a brief rapid movement of the eye between fixation points.

schema – a pattern of thought, behaviour, or experiences that organizes categories of information and the relationships among them.

theory of mind (TOM) – the ability to understand that others have beliefs that are different from yours.

Acknowledgements

Deciding which experiments to include was tricky, but I had help from half a dozen psychologists – including my wife Sue Blackmore – not to mention a philosopher, a solicitor and the postman. Then the fun started. In almost all cases I was able to go back to the original account and read about the work at first hand – a great privilege.

I have tried to explain each experiment in simple language without unnecessary jargon. Some researchers had a delightful way of putting things, while others wrote in the most impenetrable style. I have avoided technical statistics, although I do sometimes say the researchers found a significant result, meaning that it could not have happened simply by chance.

One thing that struck me repeatedly was the importance of ingenuity. A good scientist has to be focused – as Darwin was on his earthworms – but also needs to be ingenious, and imaginative.

To take a modern example, Baron-Cohen's Sally-Anne experiment was simple – needing no expensive equipment or complicated procedure – yet it delivered intriguing information about the 'theory of mind'. Similarly, Sarah-Jayne Blakemore's research on tickling generated important information about schizophrenia.

While writing this book I have learned something about experimental psychology, and a lot about human nature. I have enjoyed writing it, and I hope you enjoy reading it.

Sources

Chapter 1 Darwin, Charles. *The Formation of Vegetable Mould through the Action of Worms, with Observations of their Habits* (London: Murray, 1881).

Stratton, George M. 'Some preliminary experiments on vision without inversion of the retinal image.' *Psychological Review* 3, no. 6 (1896): 611.

Thorndike, E L. 'Animal intelligence: An experimental study of the associative processes in animals,' *Psychological Review: Monograph Supplements,* Jun 1898, 2 (4): i–109.

Pavlov, I P. 'Conditioned Reflexes: an Investigation of the Physiological Activity of the Cerebral Cortex,' trans. G. V. Anrep (London: Oxford University Press, 1927).

Perky, Cheves West. 'An experimental study of imagination.' *The American Journal of Psychology* (1910): 422–452.

Chapter 2 Watson, John B, and Rosalie Rayner. 'Conditioned emotional reactions.' *Journal of Experimental Psychology* 3, no. 1 (1920): 1.

Zeigarnik, Bluma. 'Über das Behalten von erledigten und unerledigten Handlungen,' *Psychologische Forschung,* 9 (1927): 1–85.

Bartlett, Frederic C. *Remembering: A Study in Experimental and Social Psychology* (Cambridge: Cambridge University Press, 1932).

Skinner, Burrhus Frederic.

The Behavior of Organisms: An Experimental Analysis (New York: Appleton-Century, 1938).

Roethlisberger, F J, and W J Dickson. 'Management and the worker' (Cambridge MA: Harvard University Press, 1939).

Lewin, Kurt, Ronald Lippitt, and Ralph Kw White. 'Patterns of aggressive behavior in experimentally created "social climates".' *The Journal of Social Psychology* 10, no. 2 (1939): 269–299.

Chapter 3 Tolman, Edward C. 'Cognitive maps in rats and men.' *Psychological Review* 55, no. 4 (1948): 189.

Piaget, Jean. *The origins of intelligence in children.* (New York:

International Universities Press, 1952).

Heller, M. F., and M. Bergman. 'Tinnitus aurium in normally hearing persons.' *Ann Otol Rhinol Laryngol* 62, no. 1 (1953): 73–83.

Festinger, Leon, Henry W. Riecken, and Stanley Schachter. *When Prophecy Fails: A Social and Psychological Study of a Modern Group that Predicted the Destruction of the World* (Minneapolis: University of Minnesota Press, 1956).

Asch, Solomon E. 'Studies of independence and conformity: a minority of one against a unanimous majority.' *Psychological Monographs: General and Applied* 70, No. 9, (1956): 1–70.

Harlow, Harry F., and Robert R. Zimmermann. 'The development of affectional responses in infant monkeys.' *Proceedings of the American Philosophical Society* (1958): 501–509.

Sperling, George. 'The information available in brief visual presentations.' *Psychological monographs: General and applied* 74, no. 11 (1960): 1.

Bandura, Albert, Dorothea Ross, and Sheila A. Ross. 'Transmission of aggression through imitation of aggressive models.' *The Journal of Abnormal and Social Psychology* 63, no. 3 (1961): 575.

Sherif, Muzafer, Oliver J Harvey, Jack White, William R. Hood, and Carolyn W. Sherif. *Intergroup Conflict and Cooperation: The Robbers Cave Experiment*, Vol. 10 (Norman, OK: University Book Exchange, 1961).

Chapter 4 Milgram, Stanley. 'Behavioral study of obedience.' *The Journal of Abnormal and Social Psychology* 67, no. 4 (1963): 371.

Gregory, R. L., and J. G. Wallace. 'Recovery from early blindness.' *Experimental Psychology Society Monograph* 2 (1963): 65–129.

Hess, Eckhard H. 'Attitude and pupil size.' *Scientific American*, 212, (1965): 46–54.

Hofling, Charles K., Eveline Brotzman, Sarah Dalrymple, Nancy Graves, and Chester M. Pierce. 'An experimental study in nurse-physician relationships.' *The Journal of Nervous and Mental Disease* 143, no. 2 (1966): 171–180.

Gazzaniga, Michael S. 'The split brain in man.' *Scientific American,* 217, no. 2 (1967): 24–29.

Darley, John M., and Bibb Latane. 'Bystander intervention in emergencies: diffusion of responsibility.' *Journal of Personality and Social Psychology* 8, no. 4 (1968): 377–383.

Rosenthal, Robert, and Lenore Jacobson. 'Pygmalion in the classroom.' *The Urban Review* 3, no. 1 (1968): 16–20.

Ainsworth, Mary, D. Salter, and Silvia M. Bell. 'Attachment, exploration, and separation: Illustrated by the behavior of one-year-olds in a strange situation.' *Child Development* (1970): 49–67.

Chapter 5 Zimbardo, Philip. *Stanford prison experiment.* Stanford University, 1971.

Wason, Peter C., and Diana Shapiro. 'Natural and contrived experience in a reasoning problem.' *The Quarterly Journal of Experimental Psychology* 23, no. 1 (1971): 63–71.

Rosenhan, David L. 'On being sane in insane places.' *Science* 179, no. 4070 (1973): 250–258.

Lepper, Mark R., David Greene, and Richard E. Nisbett. 'Undermining children's intrinsic interest with extrinsic reward: A test of the 'overjustification' hypothesis.' *Journal of Personality and Social Psychology* 28, no. 1 (1973): 129.

Loftus, Elizabeth F. 'Reconstructing memory: The incredible eyewitness.' *Jurimetrics J.* 15 (1974): 188.

Tversky, Amos, and Daniel Kahneman. 'Judgment under uncertainty: Heuristics and biases.' *Science* 185, no. 4157 (1974): 1124–1131.

Dutton, Donald G., and Arthur P. Aron. 'Some evidence for heightened sexual attraction under conditions of high anxiety.' *Journal of Personality and Social Psychology* 30, no. 4 (1974): 510.

Miller, William R., and Martin E. Seligman. 'Depression and learned helplessness in man.' *Journal of Abnormal Psychology* 84, no. 3 (1975): 228.

McGurk, Harry, and John MacDonald. 'Hearing lips and seeing voices.' *Nature* 264 (1976): 746–748.

Bisiach, Edoardo, and Claudio Luzzatti. 'Unilateral neglect of representational space.' *Cortex*, 14, No. 1 (1978): 129–133.

Chapter 6 Libet, Benjamin, Curtis A. Gleason, Elwood W. Wright, and Dennis K. Pearl. 'Time of conscious intention to act in relation to onset of cerebral activity (readiness-potential).' *Brain* 106, no. 3 (1983): 623–642.

Berry, Dianne C., and Donald E. Broadbent. 'On the relationship between task performance and associated verbalizable knowledge.' *The Quarterly Journal of Experimental Psychology* 36, no. 2 (1984): 209–231.

Baron-Cohen, Simon, Alan M. Leslie, and Uta Frith. 'Does the autistic child have a "theory of mind"?' *Cognition* 21, no. 1 (1985): 37–46.

Byrd, Randolph C. 'Positive therapeutic effects of intercessory prayer in a coronary care unit population.' *Southern Medical Journal* 81, no. 7 (1988): 826–829.

McNeil, Jane E., and Elizabeth K. Warrington. 'Prosopagnosia: A face-specific disorder.' *The Quarterly Journal of Experimental Psychology* 46, no. 1 (1993): 1–10.

Bem, Daryl J., and Charles Honorton. 'Does psi exist? Replicable evidence for an anomalous process of information transfer.' *Psychological Bulletin* 115, no. 1 (1994): 4–18.

Simons, Daniel J., and Daniel T. Levin. 'Failure to detect changes to people during a real-world interaction.' *Psychonomic Bulletin & Review* 5, no. 4 (1998): 644–649.

Botvinick, Matthew, and Jonathan Cohen. 'Rubber hands "feel" touch that eyes see.' *Nature* 391, no. 6669 (1998): 756–756.

Costantini, Marcello, and Patrick Haggard. 'The rubber hand illusion: sensitivity and reference frame for body ownership.' *Consciousness and Cognition* 16, no. 2 (2007): 229–240.

Blakemore, Sarah-Jayne, Daniel Wolpert, and Chris Frith. 'Why can't you tickle yourself?' *Neuroreport* 11, no. 11 (2000): R11–R16.

Ramachandran, Vilayanur S., and Edward M. Hubbard. 'Synaesthesia – a window into perception, thought and language.' *Journal of Consciousness Studies* 8, no. 12 (2001): 3–34.

Lenggenhager, Bigna, Tej Tadi, Thomas Metzinger, and Olaf Blanke. 'Video ergo sum: manipulating bodily self-consciousness.' *Science* 317, no. 5841 (2007): 1096–1099.